The Book of Appassionata

The Book of Appassionata

COLLECTED POEMS

David Citino

 OHIO STATE UNIVERSITY PRESS

COLUMBUS

Copyright © 1998 by The Ohio State University.
All rights reserved.

Library of Congress Cataloging-in-Publication Data

Citino, David, 1947–
The book of Appassionata : collected poems / David Citino.
p.   cm.
Includes index.
ISBN 0-8142-0773-1 (cl : alk. paper). — ISBN 0-8142-0774-X (pbk. : alk. paper)
I. Title.
PS3553.I86A17   1998
811'.54—dc21
98-4326
CIP

Text and jacket design by Paula Newcomb.
Type set in Stone Serif and Monotype Centaur by G & S Typesetters, Inc.
Printed by Braun-Brumfield, Inc.

The paper used in this publication meets the minimum
requirements of the American National Standard for
Information Sciences—Permanence of Paper for Printed
Library Materials. ANSI Z39.48–1992.

9 8 7 6 5 4 3 2 1

Acknowledgments

The poems in this volume appeared in the following collections:

Broken Symmetry. Columbus: Ohio State University Press, 1997.

The Weight of the Heart. Quarterly Review of Literature Poetry Book Series, vol. 35, T. Weiss and R. Weiss, eds. Princeton, N.J.: *Quarterly Review of Literature,* 1996.

The Discipline: New and Selected Poems, 1980–1992. Columbus: Ohio State University Press, 1992.

The Appassionata Lectures. Texas Review Poetry Award Chapbook. Huntsville, Tex.: *Texas Review,* 1984.

The Appassionata Doctrines. Cleveland, Ohio: Cleveland State University Poetry Center, 1986.

The Appassionata Poems. Cleveland, Ohio: Cleveland State University Poetry Center, 1983.

The following poems were reprinted in these anthologies:

"Sister Mary Appassionata Chases the Wind," in *Anthology of Magazine Verse and Yearbook of American Poetry,* Alan F. Pater, ed. Beverly Hills, Calif.: Monitor Press, 1997.

"Sister Mary Appassionata Lectures the Bible Study Class: Homage to Onan," "Sister Mary Appassionata Lectures the Eighth-Grade Boys and Girls on the Nature of the Candle," "Sister Mary Appassionata Lectures the Eighth-Grade Boys and Girls: The Family Jewels," "Sister Mary Appassionata Lectures the Folklore Class: Doctrines of the Strawberry," "Sister Mary Appassionata Lectures the Home Ec Class: The Feast," "Sister Mary Appassionata Lectures the Pre-Med Class," "Sister Mary Appassionata Lectures the Science Class: Fossils, Physics, Apple, Heart," "Sister Mary Appassionata Proves to the Entomology Class that Women and Men Descended from the Cricket," in *Upholding Mystery: An Anthology of Contemporary Christian Poetry,* David Impastato, ed. New York: Oxford University Press, 1996.

"Sister Mary Appassionata Lectures the Eighth-Grade Boys and Girls: Every Day Another Snake" and "Sister Mary Appassionata Lectures the Theology Class on the Life and Death of St. Teresa," in *The Art and Craft of Poetry,* Michael Bugeja, ed. Cincinnati, Ohio: Writer's Digest Books, 1994.

"Sister Mary Appassionata Delivers an Impromptu Speech at the Local Ponderosa" and "Sister Mary Appassionata Lectures the Science Class: Fossils, Physics, Apple, Heart," in *Odd Angles of Heaven: Contemporary Poetry by People of Faith,* David Craig and Janet McCann, eds. Wheaton, Ill.: Harold Shaw, 1994.

"Sister Mary Appassionata Lectures the Eighth-Grade Boys and Girls: Every Day Another Snake," in *Poeti Italo-Americani e Italo-Canadesi,* Ferdinando Alfonsi, ed. Catanzaro, Italy: Antonio Carello Editore, 1994.

"Sister Mary Appassionata Lectures the Sex Education Class: Doctrines of the Kiss," in *Responses to Poetry,* Alberta T. Turner, ed. New York: Longman, 1990.

"Sister Mary Appassionata Lectures the Science Class: Fossils, Physics, Apple, Heart," in *Annual Survey of American Poetry, 1986.* Great Neck, N.Y.: Poetry Anthology Press, 1987.

"Sister Mary Appassionata Lectures the Pre-Med Class," in *Anthology of Magazine Verse and Yearbook of American Poetry,* Alan F. Pater, ed. Beverly Hills, Calif.: Monitor Press, 1984.

Poems in the section "Minding the Body: New Appassionata Poems" first appeared in the following periodicals:

American Literary Review: "Sister Mary Appassionata Minds the Body."

The Critic: "Sister Mary Appassionata's Laws of Metamorphosis."

The Georgia Review: "Sister Mary Appassionata Praises Those Who Love to Watch."

Image: A Journal of the Arts and Religion: "Sister Mary Appassionata, Loving the Self," "Sister Mary Appassionata on the History of Virginity," "Sister Mary Appassionata's Concise History of Bird Droppings," and the foreword to the collection.

Laurel Review: "Sister Mary Appassionata on a Field Trip to the Columbus Zoo with the Eighth-Grade Choir" and "Sister Mary Appassionata to the Eighth-Grade Boys and Girls: Smell Considered as the Distance between Love and Love."

Madison Review: "Sister Mary Appassionata on the Birds and the Bees and the Eighth-Grade Boys and Girls."

Nebraska Review: "Sister Mary Appassionata Argues on Behalf of the Trees."

New Letters: "Sister Mary Appassionata to the Eighth-Grade Boys and Girls on the Religious History of Nakedness."

VIA: Voices in Italian Americana: "Sister Mary Appassionata on the Foreskin of the Savior."

To Sister Mary Michaeleen,
    Sister Mary Clothilde,
    Sister Mary Antonia, and
    Sister Mary Compassionata
    and all my other teachers.

Contents

VI. FEEDING THE DEAD
(*The Appassionata Doctrines,* 1983, 1986)

Foreword

I hear voices. (Don't we all?) I always have. As a typically rambunctious child I was urged to keep quiet enough so that I could hear the wisdom of my elders, but also the voices of angels, saints—the words of God himself. The prerequisite to Holiness was Silence (not Cleanliness— though that was important, too), because the silent individual could hear more easily the voices, outer and inner. Speaking always comes before writing, historically, culturally, personally. Christianity, though it is one of the "religions of the book," is more about the word *heard* than it is the word *writ*—and often the word comes by means of a little voice between the ears, what Julian Jaynes calls the "auditory hallucinations" that early women and men thought to be voices of the gods.

In my early days Roman Catholic children were not encouraged to read the Bible. The priest was there to do it aloud for them at Mass, during the reading of the Epistle and the Gospel, and the Sisters were stationed in the classroom to relay the truth. I heard God say, right out loud, "*Fiat lux*" ("Let there be light"). Noah, I was told, received instructions on boatbuilding from above. The boy Samuel, I heard, was called again and again, literally, from his bed. Moses, the priest said, stood listening to a fiery bush. Mary, it was reported, received a sudden announcement from an angel. Christ, I was told, heard a voice from heaven. I said, not read, my prayers each evening before going to bed, where I'd lie in the dark listening to Cleveland rock 'n' roll from WHK and Indians baseball games and the West Virginia Grand Ole Opry from WWVA in Wheeling. Voices. It was, all in all, no matter how still I tried to be, a noisy childhood. When I was ten, my parents bought me a transistor radio. I could carry more voices around with me.

I've been listening to Sister Mary Appassionata for some years now. She fascinates me. She is crazy, of course. Well, let me put it this way. This age of ours, as fiercely insistent as it is on believing virtually nothing, wants to apply such a label to an individual who passionately professes belief in everything. She is, at times, I believe, what I used to want to be. And she is my teacher. Yeats learned from his Crazy Jane. Both

Yeats and Jane would be unquiet in their graves if they heard me comparing myself and my teacher to them (so please keep this between us). My Crazy Mary surprises me time and again with the things I never knew, or the worlds of knowledge I've forgotten.

What seemed impossible to the child I was? Only not believing. Only nothingness. After all, I had an angel walking by my side to protect me from the legions of demons roaming northeast Ohio. My religion trained me to expect, at any moment, the mother of all miracles. God always was. Always would be. Heaven was forever and ever, Amen, as was hell. Sister Mary Appassionata is my voice of history—my personal correspondent from the country of Eternity.

Of course, she sometimes seems as if she thinks herself too wise (or at least too much the wise guy) to believe too much. There are occasions when she sounds to me like one who wants to believe the things she says but cannot, or cannot fully or without commenting wryly on the proposition before her. She seems at such times to be full of irony, as if she had embraced the doctrine and an ironic perception of this world and the other in a way that suggests that belief without a realization of the absurdity of belief in an age of unbelief is, for her, impossible—if not unbelievable. She is, I must admit, something of a puzzle, one who professes both *Faith* and *Lack of same, The way* and *No way, Hell yes* and *You've got to be kidding.*

Then, too, I may not always hear her correctly. If we've learned anything helpful from our recent critical illness, the spell of postmodernist, deconstructivist theory-fever we've suffered from over the past few decades, it is that the reader helps to create the text—the hearer alters the heard by the act of hearing, to adapt Heisenberg's Uncertainty Principle to this discussion of voices. To be honest, I'm not always certain of the borders separating us: where does the speaker leave off and the listener begin? Am I nothing more than a literary plagiarist, or are the following poems genuine collaborations? If they are collaborations, who did what?

I may, on occasion, mishear Sister Mary, or half-hear and half-create her words. I must take some responsibility for the poems, I realize, even though she deserves first billing for these performances. If the reader finds anything of merit here, then the credit should go to Appassionata herself. After all, she has all history and tradition behind her. Anything that falls short must be blamed on the one who took the dictation.

Not that she is perfect, for all her wisdom and passion. At times, I'm concerned with—embarrassed, even, by—(May I speak clearly here?)

her preoccupation with the body and its various functions. For a woman who has taken a vow of chastity, she spends a great deal of time thinking about the flesh, about the coming together of male and female in the animal and human worlds in the attempt to keep things going. Birds, angels, history, science—I can understand these interests and concerns. But she seems to me to be reading too much into the dance of generation, just as I sometimes feel she places too much importance on the fact that we are all living and dying at the same time.

Still, it is true that Mary Appassionata embraces, as I did way back when, the limitless possibility of each instant. She doesn't see a need to make distinctions among bald facts, fictions, and those fictions that could be true or once were true perfectly. She hears, I've no doubt, voices of her own. She lives her life, ranging over centuries, "unstuck in time" like Vonnegut's Billy Pilgrim. She reads the Bible, of course, but also books on church history and high energy physics and archaeology and folklore, titles like *Popular Delusions and the Madness of Crowds, A Case of Possession in Iowa, The Rhetoric of Laughter, The Story of Civilization, The Story of O, The Use of Pleasure, Lives of the Saints,* and *Lives of the Rich and Famous, The Portable Scatalog;* writers like Hildegarde of Bingen, James Joyce, Harold Robbins, Oliver Sacks; periodicals like the *New York Times, Weekly World News,* the *Globe,* the *Star*—now she even surfs the World Wide Web. And she believes (or wishes to believe) it all. She stands at the checkout line at the supermarket, accepting as gospel (or at least apocrypha) every tabloid headline and the racks full of tales of romance and lost-and-found happiness and miracle diets. "Love Changes Michael Landon's Life." I've changed greatly since my youth, but still, every once in a while, I long for the fearful, reassuring, hair-raising, goose-bumping credulities and certainties (not to mention the incredulities and uncertainties) of then. She is, I suppose, the I I think now I thought I was. She makes me free to want to believe, and to be, again, randy for miracle. She still hears the voice of God (she insists, by the way, that God too hears voices)—and, while she takes to heart all she hears, she enjoys talking back on occasion, pulling his leg, teasing and jiving and even arguing with the Creator. She has become, I suppose, my anti-self, and my altar ego.

The belief (or lack of belief) of which I speak is not only religious in nature. My sessions with Mary Appassionata make me wonder about epistemological concerns in general, ask myself how I've come to accept and know the things I lay claim to. How much have I learned myself? Very little, I fear. I have had to take nearly everything on authority, I must admit. Can I prove to my own satisfaction, by my own lights, the truth of evolution, the existence of a menagerie of subatomic particles, the reality of black holes, the documentary hypothesis of biblical authorship and transmission? I've had to rely so much on the knowing, the belief, of others, just as the believer relies on the authority, say, of the scribes and evangelists—and the voices. Have I filled the void left by the loss of belief with purely materialistic entities? What resides, in her and in me, where an undiluted faith once abided? Reason? Science? Cynicism? Her answers inspire in me a host of questions; her questions lead me to search for answers.

Mary Appassionata is a composite, yes, of those otherworldly ones who wished to communicate truth to me, but she is also a blend of the flesh-and-blood teachers and mentors I've had in my life. I'm fifty as I write this, a poet-teacher by profession, which means that I've been in school for forty-five years—grades K through 45. So many bells of the season, ringing the changes of rooms. Period after period of books, words bouncing off walls, mingling with chalk dust. Term after term of recitation, exercise, review, attempted comprehension. Trial and error, inculcating, suggesting, informing, persuading. All my life, nearly, I've tried to move around the room in the square dance of the Socratic method. It occurs to me that while so much time had to be taken up in the early classroom years with enforcing order, order is always a major concern of the poet and the teacher, whether it be the instilling of a new order or the overturning of the old.

Teaching, like poetry, is a demanding master or mistress to the practitioner who operates in a conscientious manner. Both professions can be infinitely arduous. A poet seeks to know something, and labors to transmit that knowing to others. Art is the lesson learned in the school of hard knocks, a method of attempted discovery, the attempted discovery itself, the report of success or failure. For every uplifting, so many downers. If there is another profession as noble and debasing as that of the poet, it is that of the teacher—if they're not in fact one and the same.

Of the four sisters—the four graces, I could say—to whom the present volume is dedicated, the first three, Sisters Mary Michaeleen and Clothilde and Antonia, members of the Religious Sisters of Mercy, actually were teachers of mine at Ascension of Our Lord Elementary School in Cleveland. I remember them vividly. Their makeup-free faces framed in wimples and veils, foreheads wrinkling in smiles or exasperation, the thick black belts from which hung great clacking rosaries, the magnificent nuns' shoes, as stolid, functional, and architecturally complex and improbable as their medieval beliefs.

The fourth woman, Sister Mary Compassionata, I've never met. She came to me out of the blue—I'm perfectly serious—in just the sort of voice from above of which I've been speaking. She was a nurse, a Sister of the Holy Cross at Mount Carmel Hospital in Columbus, where my wife has worked for years. I heard her name being paged on a day twenty-five years ago when I was there to pick up Mary at the end of the day. "Sister Mary Compassionata," the disembodied voice through the sound system said, over and over. What? The Compassionate One? A name that suggested a life devoted to a virtue as humanly necessary, and as close to love, as compassion? Having compassion was her job. She stood for it, surrounded as she was by examples of human suffering and imperfection. I saw her—perhaps she saw herself—as an explorer of this virtue, as its embodiment, its emblem. I actually felt, at that moment, that I might be inspired by what I was hearing. It was an urgent call. I began to consider the possibilities. I had an idea.

I

Minding the Body
New Appassionata Poems

Sister Mary Appassionata
to the Eighth-Grade Boys and Girls
on the Religious History of Nakedness

A slither, a hiss,
the spitting out of seeds
all down the front,
and Eve and Adam
saw through one another.

Noah cursed the son
who eyed him passed out
in his birthday suit purpled
with wine, and Israel
had an enemy forever.

David unzipped, got
happy feet and, dancing
a good sweat before God
and the servant girls,
lost his head, his wife.

Susanna, so pretty and hot.
She got a rise out of
those old spying guys
by laving smooth limbs
in a sultry garden.

Jesus was nude only
three times in thirty-three years —
you can look it up:
in the manger, on the cross,
in the tomb, teaching us

every bath-time we're
baby, lover, corpse,
savage again, victim

of torture, figure of devotion,
rolls and poles of flesh.

We're taken out
the way we come in,
wrinkled, bewildered,
wondering where in the hell,
with nothing much to hide.

Sister Mary Appassionata Argues
on Behalf of the Trees

They mean three things: once
upon a time we could fly;
it's easy to fall a long way;
we rise only by pulling our weight.

They stand to dare the wind,
lightning, blight. They fall
to make more space
between dark and the light.

They're lithe girls dancing,
shaking wet hair; women,
strong-footed, beautifully thick
of hip and thigh. When

we came down the trunk,
vagina slid forward, penis
grew. We stood straight,
four hands freed for labor

and loving face to face.
Monkeys show how once
we danced through planets,
swayed with variable winds.

DNA flourishes in us,
gnarled story writhing out
root, bud, bloom, hue and cry.
A way to kill and cook God,

to grow back to Eden,
lush corolla igniting a life
to kindling, ember, ash.
Boats to float the soul.

*Sister Mary Appassionata on the Foreskin
of the Savior*

Fascinating, we say today,
from Latin *fascinum,*
the angelic little god
hugely, devilishly erect

you can handle tonight
at Pompeii, to poke out evil eyes
or get knocked up, if that's
your desire—and what,

with the possible exception
of a divine and cosmic *Hers,*
can be more enthralling
than an eternally stone-hard *His?*

Zeus chose the swan and bull
because they're really hung.
A thousand Renaissance churches
claimed to own a piece

of the Redeemer's precious prepuce,
granddaddy of all relics,
it being the only mortal part
he didn't take with him

on the trip back home
to the seventh heaven.
Look at the many paintings,
Madonna and Child, Mary parting

the Bambino's swaddling clothes
with a knowing Mona Lisa smile,

or read the stories in The Book,
Genesis through Revelation,

Eve, Lot's wife, the mother
of the baby Solomon tried
to halve, Mary Magdalene:
the God of all of us is all man.

Sister Mary Appassionata
on the History of Virginity

Nuns in the Middle Ages—
that is to say, back then,
not older ones nowadays—
thought they'd get pregnant
if the Savior thought of them.

Mary was thought, after all,
to be a virgin until He came,
then she was not—Joseph
red in the face—but
the world reveres her still,

as it often does those
who do a thing unthinkable,
not for what she was to become,
but what it thinks
she forever used to be.

Sister Mary Appassionata to the Fourth-Year Latin Class:
Membrum et semen diaboli frigida sicut glacies

The devil's member and semen are cold as ice.

You can look it up. Witches, shivering
through broomstick nights, nipples aching
with herbal oils, know the demon moving inside
as purest cold. Then you've got your angels,

made of fire. No matter how hard they try,
they can't make it with one another
without burning holes in the clouds. Humans
are magic to them, weighty works of art.

They watch as we go at it in our rituals
of two, bodies winding in sweaty sheets,
breathing sigh of sighs, cries and moans,
ragged breath the symphony of creation.

Too much evil, too much good is a weather
too severe for love. We ache for one another
because the lover's body is a temperate zone,
enough ice and fire to make us forget, briefly,
we were not made to freeze or burn or fly.

Sister Mary Appassionata, Bird-Watching
with the Eighth-Grade Boys and Girls

We have too much in common.
Because we once shared the trees,
the soughing whisper of leaves

means peace to us, mortal dangers—
gravity, wind, snake—are unseen,
and our language of love and war

is the same old song. Goshawks
come together six hundred times per clutch
of eggs, skylarks only once: some lovers

are more assiduous than others.
Because the male bird of prey
is so long away from home, and thus

can't keep his mate from other males,
when he returns he mounts her
like mad, trying to dilute the memory

of any hardened rival. As day grows
and new light throbs through trees,
the testes of male and female

swell to hundreds of times their size.
Like ours, their bodies announce when
it's time to have nothing else in mind,

because there's something greater
than any living thing alone. Feathers
and clothes are for preening, purely

for show—and to hide our true designs.

Sister Mary Appassionata on the Birds and the Bees and the Eighth-Grade Boys and Girls

A million teeming species
getting it on, rocking the world—
it makes you faint to think.

Demons, fairies, killer bees
defy gravity; our finny friends,
mermen and maids, roiling calamari

heave seven seas, churn streams;
unicorns, minotaurs, weasels even
get down to it on terra firma.

Humans do it anywhere they can,
give it up to save their skins,
make the race last long after

the soul plummets into bony throes
of night neuter and unmoaning.
Beasts know one way to paradise.

It's back-to-back, belly-to-belly
for bugs, male posterior for goat.
Archangels tongue wanton psalms

in one another's ear, waft with
languid wings, sweating nearly.
Humans, more substantial, writhe

every alphabet into texts of desire.
You've come a long way, you hominids
standing erect with opposable thumbs,

the world's history in your hands,
your genes, hearts thundering,
minds in the gutter again and again.

Sister Mary Appassionata's Concise History
of Bird Droppings

Birds (unlike angels—who, when
they move, lose only light,
on which they've feasted overmuch)
are songs of what they eat.

The droppings of granivores
are hard as can be, their singing
a field of sharp cries,
while those of frugivores

run sweet, loosely indolent,
free from care and strain,
their notes the airiest of all,
passing through air with ease.

Droppings of insectivores
depend on what bugs
have happened by, sweet worm,
tart beetle, fly or fire ant.

We're talking, in some cases,
prodigious pyramids of the past.
Roosting passenger pigeons
buried millions of acres

of forest understory; now they
coo ghost-warnings of the sin
of taking for granted
what we feel is beneath us.

Waste not, want not; like
the (dumb) bunny rabbit,

some birds, poring over the past
instead of the present, recycle.

The replacement of 25%
of cattle feed with chicken manure
has proven nutritionally—
if not aesthetically—sound.

Some birds let fly to show us
and our shiny cars what they think
of what we've done to water,
fields, woods, their very air,

as lesser black-backed gulls
dive-bomb a predator.
Moving keeps us, too, in health,
takes out some aggression.

The Master Mover made us
and the apple, so with regularity
we feel the urge to look below
whither we come from and go,

the difference between us
and the dark, cooling soil,
to know what marvels we are,
and how, light again, we rise.

Sister Mary Appassionata
to the Eighth-Grade Boys and Girls:
Smell Considered as the Distance
between Love and Love

Here's a lesson in higher math,
you little stinkers, hormones wafting
around the classroom: all boy dogs
for three miles come running
for the sudden heat of one bitch;

it takes a garden hose to sunder
what two odorous souls join together,
centuries of domesticity chased
by glassy-eyed yelp and growl.
When the merest breeze calls—

a dainty speck of pheromone
on the tip of throbbing abdomen
of lady monarch—a male
acres away stiffens wings
and lifts against all odds.

To the sow in the mood
the boar's fuming breath
is an hour of finest truffles.
For any of us love-mammals, despite
what we've seen in blue movie,

size doesn't count. Males
with the finest scents—
not implements—shrivel
the ardor of other suitors
and gain the precious prize.

A male lemur blasts his aroma
at another while beating
himself on the head

with his tail, as if the urge
to create were an instrument

blunt enough to knock him silly,
the love-song of smell
coaxing us out of the family tree
to ensure, lap upon lap, heat
after heat, the race, the chase, go on.

Sister Mary Appassionata Praises Those Who Love to Watch

These late scores just in:
in two hours, two randy rats did it
244 times, then collapsed,
a new rodent world record, while

one slow dance lasted a year
for a pair of pythons —
talk about commitment
to making a relationship work.

Go figure. Apostle birds stay
chaste until twelve assemble —
there's safety in numbers.
Palolo worms behave until

neap tide the last quarter moon
of October and November.
Want drives our calendar, too.
History means who did whom

how often. Women bleed
under horned, heaving moons;
men are made to help them
make the ocean motion.

It all happens on our watch,
a show, a passionate math,
desperate, avid roiling of seas,
birds humping in lustful trees.

No Twelve-Steps can kick
this addiction, a ticking desire,
a lust to count the ways
of love's numberless wonders.

Sister Mary Appassionata on a Field Trip
to the Columbus Zoo with the Eighth-Grade Choir

Count off, young ones, two by two.
No more solos: you're ready for duet,
fingers twisting in sweaty palms.

So the tragic, comic opera gets sung.
Listen as walrus and seal trumpet out
bellows of lonely ache, fathom

after loud fathom, from the diaphragm
of the soul through seas of grief,
just to teach us how to yearn.

Eve and Adam sang every position
under God's leering eye, until
they invented the mortal alphabet.

Mosquitoes kazoo out three love songs
the human ear can't bloody hear,
passion's prickly itch and smack.

The bull canary rears back and trills
his pretty mate's ovaries awake.
So the music of our mortal *Two, Two*

sets the weeds and stars to rocking,
every word and sigh a song of love,
our divine beastly human airs.

Sister Mary Appassionata's Laws of Metamorphosis

Girls if they're not careful
sitting with arms and legs uncrossed
too near their dreams in technicolor dark
can be changed into goddesses
with great breasts, desperate breaths;

boys too easily become wolves
or giant octopi or throbbing flies.
Sin itself can fall from any alien world,
cause a row of buttons to open, one by one,
slither out of black lagoon or popcorn box.

Heroes of a child-bright Bronze Age
too soon will be cast into statues
to lord it over legions of pigeons
and the poor, growing unrecognizable
from tarnish, a patina of urban dirt.

Profit can transmute purest air
to sulfur dioxide, rush of trout stream
to Love Canal, slick and sludge fuming
like purgatory, iron infrastructures
to palsied filigrees of utter rust.

Childhood heavens, infinite realms
of imagination and light, shrink
to space the flag of any nation can claim
to claim, armed satellites careening
among the stars of every creed.

Grandfathers become bellowing pains
just in time. Any mother can change

her name to Cancer. Too many fathers
grow to sudden ghosts, doubled over
by stroke or that final broken heart.

Sister Mary Appassionata Addresses
the Ohio Supreme Court

One of your law-and-order men, Hammurabi.
If an infant died in the care of a wet nurse,
her breasts were cut off, the sentence praised

as double justice: not only the pain, she had
to find another line of work. In the Bible,
how many women show up only to be wrong,

breed or die—sometimes all three? Solomon
was so hot to hack a babe in half, it couldn't
have been a boy. In our own scarlet cities,

fear hangs out in bedroom, parking garage,
behind Door Number One, Two, Three—
the batterer freed to hiss, *I can't have you,*

no one can. Still today beards in old robes
intone, *You've no right. You'll do what*
you're told. You'll carry this baby to term.
You must. It's just, the law.

Sister Mary Appassionata Minds the Body

1.

Socrates, past his prime, moving into the Wrinkle Room,
starting to sag, advised young ones to look often
into mirrors, so that, learning by heart
the unspeakable, hurt-in-the-throat beauty of youth,
they'd strive in the time remaining to make themselves worthy.
So often sadness makes us wise.

2.

The earth is haunted, curse and hex glowing from stone, bone,
carapace and wing everywhere we walk. Is there a site
to put the foot where some life hasn't tripped,
enriching, fouling the soil? Dirt is Great Grandfather.
Everywhere we stand on Grandmother's grave.

3.

The sadist and masochist are alchemists of the body,
transmuting joy to pain for other or self, thinking beauty
in blindfolds, sighs in gags, dances in ropes—and believing
so fervently in artifice they come to feign the truth.

4.

Can heaven and hell take another soul? Where are the numbers
we need to crunch to know? How much guilt, for bringing
into the world another body and soul with their cavities
of profligate need? We'll pay for this lust to divide.

With our very lives.

Sister Mary Appassionata, Loving the Self

This morning again,
as I wash my face:
those eyes, that mouth.
The courtship begins anew

in the steamy mirror,
a gaze nearly copulatory,
reptilian and limbic brains
whispering *You're living*

forever, Love, despite
what the cortex knows
about space and time. Here
all desire begins; here

will it end. The least
I need, another end to night,
light dilating the pupils.
Researchers know eighteen

different human smiles,
ways of saying to mirror,
lover, other, *I mean you
no harm.* The brain,

three-pound honeydew history
of the world, admiring itself.
There's but one way out
of this mad, passionate affair,

when you think about it.
Whitman's brain splattered

on the floor of the lab
of the American Psychometric Society

when a technician, calculating
the capacity of brute desire—
one brain estimating another—
stumbled. Can the body

allow a mind to conceive
of a thing beyond itself?
The awful fall, a universe
tumbling toward dissolution,

ripe fruit flung by gravity
at dark once again. I smile
to, at, myself. Saved by dawn,
habitual act of love, I'm back.

II

The Excommunication
of the Locusts
from Broken Symmetry

Sister Mary Appassionata Chases the Wind

Walk out into this industrial wind
and it hits you: we're eroding.
Even the light is dirty.
We can't tell what is or isn't us,
immune systems growing confused.

Think of Pandora's nasties wafting
like rotten pollen on the thermals,
fanged angels with bat faces
flapping above Egypt's nurseries,
ill winds blowing everybody bad.

It's not that we've not tried
to stop it. Ethiopians sliced
at the wind with shining knives.
Eskimo women swung clubs
to chase bony cold from the hearth.

Herodotus praised the African army
that marched into desert
behind cymbal and drum
to drive away deadly drought,
but it lured them on, turned

on them and now they lean at rest
in the sandstorm of forever.
Pliny the Elder thought it
the breath of stars
until Vesuvius burned his ass.

Tonight it shakes the moon,
brandishes oak and ash at heaven,

Orion lurching like a drunk,
the air bright knives, warnings,
the winds of angry angels.

Sister Mary Appassionata on the Excommunication
of the Locusts

In Paris, a cock swollen with pride
forgot his place and committed
the *Heinous and unnatural crime against*
God and man of laying an egg.
He was bound to the stake and burned,

the pungent scents of the sentence
teaching the poor a truth
concerning the unappeasable appetite
for crisply executed justice
of those who cling to power.

Cows and sows and ewes who'd allowed
themselves to be sweet-talked
by lonely masters, positioned above them—
or behind—by the Master-Maker,
suffered the lash, lost their heads.

Hungry mosquitoes, horseflies,
locusts and weevils and bees,
even man's best friends, who'd let it slip
their minds that they were fashioned
but to serve, were excommunicated.

A sow appeared in 1386 before
the Falaise tribunal, and counsel
provided by the court argued with success
that since both swinish and human hungers
were created by the all-wise Master,

there'd been no sin, unless He—the He
Who Made Us—had made a mortal mistake.
Still, she'd eaten a human baby,

a sin if ever there was one,
so the sow was sternly lectured

by the judges—firmly officious
in flowing robes and scowls—who told her
that while she'd overstepped the bounds
even of beastliness, she'd have gotten off
if she hadn't given in to this yen

on Friday, on which the Savior
has suspended His decree of our dominion
over beast and fowl and ordered
*This day thou shalt not put teeth
to meat.* The sentence was capital.

After a priest heard her confession
and administered chrism and holy water
she was tortured, then held in a cell
with the worst of her human peers,
fed on the finest swill at public expense,

and hanged with full ceremony on the square,
such rite serving as eloquent deterrence
to any beast who had thoughts of
yanking the great chain of being,
putting, before the horse, the cart.

Sister Mary Appassionata Announces
the Winning Project in the Eighth-Grade Science Fair:
Our Good Friends the Insects

A bug for every ailment, so
we lovers can go on forever.
Royal jelly keeps a body light;
not one beekeeper in the history
of honey has known impotence or gout.
Mosquitoes can draw out paresis,
final throes of V.D. and give
curable yellow fever in return.

Only King Roach ever was, will be.
Even earthworms are D.P.'s,
our natives having been iced
by glaciers, the newcomers sailing
in potted plants of Pilgrims.
Burrowing into prairie and bog,
they loved themselves until they came
to eat and excrete a continent.

Termites, ants, swarming gnats
can be baked in tasty cakes,
but let me recommend our special:
tender grasshopper nuggets.
Chinese ladies kept cicadas
in dainty jade cages, chewed food
for them, dished out on porcelain,
slept to love's timeless chiming.

At night, spread a muslin cloth
around an ash that smells of mice—
their scent. Shake the branches,
and the iridescent beetles, too cold
to flee, will drop from heaven
like manna. Hippocrates found

that, ground, they cured dropsy
and scratched a thousand other itches,

but every teen knows *cantharides*
as the Spanish fly that can
make a man feverish enough to force
a groundhog hole or ironwood knot,
drive a woman so mad she'll try
Oh, the big fat candle of desire,
breathless, *Oh,* wild ride,
the knobbed gearshift of love.

Sister Mary Appassionata to the Chamber of Commerce:
Remains of Earliest Hominid Discovered in Ruins of Atlantis
under Lake Erie

Imagine your lost daughter,
lips glaring like refinery flares,
crack rocks and douche bottle
heavy in her purse, coming on

to pillars of the community
on a neon street. *Hey now,*
Mister, knees of hose ruined
as she kneels, slow rhythm

of hand and head, up, down,
before an idling BMW, up, down,
gulp of bitter poison,
the awful groaning stillness.

We're killing her, you see?
Or your grandmother, gumming
the hard wad of Doublemint
she found under a potted plant

at the glorious Galleria
before she was booted out,
lying under cardboard before
the AmeriTrust atrium.

Or your own Appalachian mamma
in day-glo pasties, back
still stiff and proud
in the honky-tonk mirror

as she humps the disco pole,
her kids in mortal fear

of the boyfriend back home.
Goddesses of our cities.

Atlantis, she's another story:
state of the feminine we
knew enough to worship
long away and far ago, pure

as hoarfrost beyond the suburbs,
no citizens whining, *But
how much will a just world
cost us? How damn much?*

O City Fathers, on Public Square
let us float municipal bonds
and build an underwater park
to honor her, trees, a statue

anatomically correct, a plaque:
*Here lies Mother. On this spot
the goddess wound up our sexes
like bedroom alarms and set us off.*

She lies untarred by the lake
of commerce, slough of this
our daily effluent. Let us
resurrect her by moving as one,

our caring for one another
the one prayer she'll hear.
Let us heed her cries, moans
of double-helixed generation

whorling from her pretty shell,
passion's splash and ooze,
love honest and equal,
water music, heart's blood.

Sister Mary Appassionata Explicates a Graffito
for the Eighth-Grade Boys

Don't look up here for a joke.
It's in your hand.

Little old man wearing a rain hat.
He's got a mind of his own:
stands up to anything, but
finding home, he cries and cries.
Lies down and dies.

Stings, then like a drone
expires just to sweeten the honey.

So damn polite. He bows,
loyal family retainer minding
his manners, but suddenly
a puppet Punch chasing each Judy.

When you must be chaste?
Foams like a mad dog.

The old snake in the grass,
but holier than thou
the morning after, burning
from every indiscretion.

After all, he's your life.
And he'll be the death of you.

Time after time he rises
from bed faithful as dawn,
as if love were
the only mortal reason
to say to night *Not yet.*

Sister Mary Appassionata, Marriage Counselor

Constancy is for the birds: 92%
twitter and flit the joys
of the faithful married life.

Mourning doves, e.g., pair off
till Death do they part,
hoot out matins and lauds

in crack-of-dawn duets,
bill and coo on wires running
taut above the two-lane

the blessings of staying put.
But in the teeming barnyard
a single gobbling Tom

will strut through scores
of moaning, lovey-dovey hens.
Flushed female chimps breathless

with estrus choose to stoop
before all male comers;
and a whole day's worth

of frantic chest drumming
by the hairy bull gorilla
can't keep his ladies

from climbing other trees
to peel forbidden fruit.
So go figure. The Creator

wishes us to keep all but one
field fallow, or wants us
to sow some wider, wilder oats;

or, chaste and single forever
yet having a son with an eye
for the ladies, He can't decide,

and this uncertainty makes
history, the scorecard of love,
our world of joy and woe.

Sister Mary Appassionata on the History of Madness

It all began in water.
Diodorus of Sicily discovered
the African lake whose waters
bubbled through souls of those
who drank, making them babble
every sin they'd hid,

and Pliny's spring in Asia Minor
loved by Apollo, its chill
driving bathers crazy enough
to know all things
but too much knowing dragging them
like lead to the oozy bottom.

The man who disrupted Mass
by lifting skirts of devout maidens
during the elevation of the Host
was no lunatic, though
Thomas More had him flogged
to teach what passion costs,

believers caught too often
with heads in cloud and bodies
immersed in the elements,
hell flaring from frictions
of heart and soul, divine match
struck on rough-hewn human stone.

In Germany, the Dancing Mania,
perjurers held right hands raised,
fingers of the left crossed
as they danced and whirled.

Adulterers lay writhing, moaning
on bellies and backs, every position.

On June 26, 1428, a monk
driven by the demons of loneliness
began to dance and when he'd used up
every inch of his cell, he died.
Even a timid mystic is aberrant
in this bloody literal world.

When we conceive too narrowly,
nothing connects. Orson Welles
proved what the ancients knew well,
that looking up on an uncloudy night
can make the soul confuse
the truly beautiful and true.

Faith is the essence of insanity,
Paul knew, all that's hoped for,
everything unseen. If we ache
only for what is, we're nothing
but the torn-winged wren
fluttering near time's fierce cat.

III   *The Cholesterol Levels of the Gods*
from The Weight of
the Heart

*Sister Mary Appassionata on
the Nature of the Hero*

Arthur whips sword from stone;
Rama takes up the great bow.
Mary squishes the snake's head
with her pretty, immaculate heel;
Madame Curie just glows.

Odysseus pokes his fear
in its one eye; Columbus,
for all his glistering greed,
lashes himself to the mast
to weather gales of doubt.

Bright as Hermes, Roadrunner
dusts Coyote at light speed.
Nolan Ryan ices a magic arm,
climbs the mound to hurl
heat at the Angel of Age.

Isis, offering her breast
to baby Horus, becomes
Madonna with pudgy Bambino;
Pharaoh ascends his throne,
the lap of the goddess of death.

Daniel nails the old lechers
who came on to Susanna, while
the Manhattan prosecutor,
that Giuliani guy, asks
just the right questions to slam

the cell door on pinky-ringed,
hard-on neighborhood boys.
My heroes! You're something,

you know, laddering
up Sinai, K2 and Matterhorn

or strolling moony seas,
centuries of mortal contention
with lion, swan and bull,
but even more, you're
the daunting dare hurled

at some mangy private demon,
the taut-lipped *I'll change
this life,* the stilling
of a clamorous self, pure merge
of temporal wish and will

into a shining timeless deed.

Sister Mary Appassionata Praises
the Sense of Smell

Houses and rooms are full of perfumes.
    —Walt Whitman

Lion and lamb, lion's den
and sheep pen, ardor of Adam
and Eve's sweet cunning fruit—
only nothing smells the same.
To safely make it through
this blooming, awful world
we must sniff out the difference.

Teachers live longer, inhaling,
every period, youth's essence,
lessons licorice-sweet,
salt of dew on downy lip,
chalk dust erasing wrinkles,
chafe of damp corduroy,
ringing change of the hour.

Socrates knew a new bride
needs no perfume but innocence.
And not just beauty speaks.
Power too breathes out
its name: while his armies
blackened earth, Great Alexander
stank of blood and violets;

after noon, the left armpit
of a certain nobleman of Paris
exuded a priceless musk—
you can look it up. Sorrow
takes away all sense of smell,
anger offends like the flare
of sulfurous lucifer match.

History's a dog-eared tome, sheaves
of mildew. Scratch and sniff:
St. Thérèse showering roses on us
from above; that stench which says
Sin Here; baby's sweet, sour kiss,
the insult of ammoniac age,
our bouquet of every day.

Sister Mary Appassionata to the Editor
of the Columbus Dispatch

Since 1830, the pope's signed off on
only seven appearances of Mary.
She fancies Western Europe:
Portugal's Fatima; France, at
Lourdes, the rue de Bac in Paris,
La Salette, Pontmain;
Belgium's Beauraing and Banneux.

At Fatima, the year Lenin whacked
the tsar, breathless Mary announced
that the 1917 Red machine
would mean a heap of trouble
but then go up in smoke, fumes
of a vodka coup, unrumbling tanks
in 1991. It's all come true.

The local bishop makes the call,
whether Mary has dropped in
for real or no. She hasn't been,
skeptics say, to Lubbock, where
rosaries riot every Crayola hue;
nor to Bayside, where her X-ray eyes
expose the pope as a Rich Little fake;

not to Medjugorje, where the bishop,
his land loud with tribal death,
wants to check the I.D. of someone
billed as "The Queen of Peace";
and not to Youngstown, where
the sun pulses like a fat old heart
although the mills are cold.

She visits only the holy lonely,
teenage girls already aroused
by other miracles—bitter and bright
as blood—and dying to believe
a mother can remain intact,
assume her heaven without
going the loose grave way.

It's no accident that the Institute
for Marian Research sits near
Wright-Patterson A.F.B. in Dayton,
where sleep those frozen beings
the world insists UFO'd from Venus
but who, if the truth be told,
wear folded wings and broken halos.

Downed in a fierce dogfight
with scrambled Ohio flyboys over
Route 40 on their way to herald
Mary's next scheduled gig,
they prove the tight-minded folly
of those who, wide-eyed, live
to doubt. You don't buy it?

It's your funeral. Walk out
on a clear night. They light
every radar screen. Dominions,
Thrones in formation, bogeys,
pitchforks gleaming, at nine o'clock.
The Holy House flew all the way
from Nazareth to Loretto,

spinning like Dorothy's, to squish
the witch of our unimagining.
Heavenly beings rise and soar,
barrel roll, peel off, stack up
over O'Hare, and sometimes fall
to earth. Remember Joshua,
The Day the Earth Stood Still?

*Walking by the Lion's Den Adult Theater
and Bookstore, Sister Mary Appassionata
Experiences the Stigmata*

This thought like a red light,
gash of crimson salty as
fuming seas we struggled from:

loving ourselves, we bleed as one.
A baby wails in a mess of red;
we buy a washer and dryer

and live forever. Blame it
on the blood. One half
of all stigmatics are Italian,

Francis of Assisi the very first.
It could be—not a few
serious scientists claim—

that those operatically cursed
with the five puncture wounds
(read it and weep: four nails, one spear)

are bleeding hearts who think
themselves a drop too holy.
God dropped a heavy house on

Blessed Bloody Dodo of Frisia.
The *Dunstable Annals* tattle on
the man who nailed himself to a tree

at fairs, staining crowds below.
The Oxford Council staunched him.
He got life, a room with a pulse.

But blood's the wonder. Domenica
of Paradise ate only white wafers
twenty long years, although

she daily sparred with demons
and bled like a punch-drunk pug.
Francesca de Serrone's blood

stank of fresh violets and ran
hot enough to blister the fingers
of the hoo-hawing gawkers.

Walk into the furtive cinema
on Ladies' Night and watch
the paper bags and popcorn boxes

tick and throb in sparkling dark
in the laps of rapt believers,
god-smooth bodies on the screen

dancing, panting to raise a sweat,
and tell me love's not in the blood
and there's no miracle to us,

wounds to this flesh, no scarlet cord
binding together soul, mind
and the loud, travailing heart.

Sister Mary Appassionata on the
Cholesterol Levels of the Gods

They won't eat their vegetables.
Only Italian saints merit
pasta and polenta in paradise.
And how do you get a being
who's All-Everything to exercise?

In the Eumaeus of the *Odyssey,*
after the boar is stunned,
its bristles, bones, fat
and chine were barbecued
for Hermes and the nymphs.

The gods lust for more
than one kind of sweetmeat—
if you get my drift.
It's a wonder there are
leftovers for us mortals.

They like nothing better
than times of spitting fire,
the lean, bloody pious praying
loud over crackles of fat,
wreaths of greasy smoke.

Yahweh too liked his meat
charred and rare, tons
of roast bull and dove.
Also two-legged critters,
tribe upon wailing tribe.

Aztec Prime Rib of Human came
with tomatoes and peppers—
on a bed of gold maize,

for presentation. In time
we love every god to death.

Pythagoras, though he reverenced
everything alive, after
he'd discovered that the square
of the hypotenuse
of a right triangle

equals the sum of the square
of the other sides, axed
a hecatomb of oxen—
one hundred bawling, shitting beasts.
A fine mess we make of belief.

IV *Notes toward the Perfection of Sex from* The Discipline

Sister Mary Appassionata's Homage
to St. Einstein

Continents drift each year
three centimeters farther from Pangaea,
our pampered playpen Eden
where every beast could speak as well
as Woody Hayes or Bishop Sheen,
every tree could mean
a shade of difference
and we were oh, so whole.
Our days are legs of the journey
from love's Big Bang
Mother and Daddy set off,
our minds and all that's in our genes
remnants of the blast
flung to corners of the universe.
Rubbing limbs together, still
we try to keep that spark alive,
imitating all of their positions,
until we come to the last.

Of the planets, only Venus
spins counterclockwise,
thus lovers don't grow old
yet never seem to have the time.
Earth's atmosphere stands
four times taller than Everest,
a weight enough to slow
our bias by $\frac{1}{1000}$ of a second
a day. We eat, drink, breathe
each moment, relatively.
St. Einstein made us a universe
that curves near any heavenly mass,
which illustrates that,
unattached, out of context,

we don't mean a damn thing.
Our very myths, patterned
above us in the darkening sky,
depend on where we stand.

Sister Mary Appassionata, on Hearing
that Kant Disregarded the Sense of
Smell Purely on Aesthetic Grounds

Well, that's fine for him, but how
to explain sanctity's odor,
St. Thérèse showering the world
with fluttering ghosts of roses,
the monk of Prague who could sniff out
folks who played around?

And another thing. The truth
about blondes? It's their souls—
they're different perfumes.
A sultan would choose each night
from the love letters of clothing
sent from the harem's spice garden.

Goethe confessed he once stole
Madame von Stein's bodice
so that, inspired, he could sing her
into being like a poem; Henri III
found love after playing Blind Man's Bluff
with the linen of Mary of Cleves.

In Borneo as in Casablanca a *kiss*
is just a *smell.* But watch where you
put your nose. Nero's dinner guests
smothered under tons of flowers.
An Indian queen sent Great Alexander
a lovely slave girl trained

in the arts of love who carried
deadly poison under her arms.
The dour, sour Puritans passed laws
against inhaling too close

to the opposite sex. And another thing.
At the Black Assizes at Oxford

all who sat downwind of the prisoners
died within forty hours. But
we know it's truly an ill wind
that blows good nobody's way.
The good ship *Arthur,* bearing two tons
of excrement from Guadeloupe,

lost its crew one by one
to the great floating waste of life,
sailed into Nice a ghost ship
piloted only by sated flies
too heavy even to rise,
ready to bring the world to bloom.

Chemists can make twenty-one flavors
of musk, so while the Asian deer
may be close to extinct, humans
are in no immediate danger.
Scents of love can conquer all,
angels wafting over earth to trumpet

the sweet meaty beastliness of us.

In a Clearing Hacked out of the Rain
Forest, Sister Mary Appassionata
Lectures the Young Cannibals

Well, it's God's best recipe,
I'll agree, a manna far surpassing
jerky, chicken nuggets, corn dogs.

But why not do it figuratively,
love-bites of a savior's heart?
Not the bloody literal Lugosi-thing

you do. High atop the pyramid,
steps slick all the way down
with a Niagara of clotted gore,

the Aztec priest wrenched
the love-muscle, held it high,
a throbbing bird in the hand.

In Old Testament times
it was a riptide of blood,
what with all the Canaanites,

butchered oxen and doves.
The circumciser sucked hard
to staunch the flow. Now *there's*

a covenant. Only be beyond
the carnal. Mouths house
the soul of us, shivery tongue-flutter,

tickle of hummingbird, prickly kiss.
We can develop too great a taste.
Napoleon in frozen Russia fed

his men Hardtack of Fallen Comrade.
And those Andes rugby boys,
Alferd Packer and the Donner party—

if only they'd refused to bite
the very hands that fed them,
the too-human communion.

Some feasts should be too dear.
Look around you: life's lushness,
calf, pheasant, suckling pig,

fragile bounty of a perfect earth,
wisps of finite air misting
in the greenhouse of our world.

When we live only for our appetites,
like Cronus, daddy guppies, cats,
it's our own children we devour.

Sister Mary Appassionata Delivers
an Impromptu Speech at the
Local Ponderosa

Go right ahead. Gorge beasts
on grain, and feed in turn
on beasts. Nine of every ten
calories involved, *you lose.*

Hindus say 330,000,000 gods
in the body of each cow.
In India alone, 180,000,000 cows.
Go figure how many that makes,

each mad as hell about some sin,
venial or mortal, a bureaucrat
insisting His or Her version
Is, Was and *Forever Shall,*

whining over calendar or tithe.
No way you'll please them all.
What's there to do to live
the good life but do without?

The Talmud claims the demons
in this world number 7,495,926,
bellies fat with sin, barely
enough to go around NYC,

much less gird the globe.
Surely we're underestimating
the enemy's troop strength.
Thank God an unhungry angel

walks with each of us.
We've a holy war on our hands.

Pigs get hungry enough,
they'll eat anything—

one another even. But go
to the Jains, who seal up bugs
by the millions in temple rooms
amid enormous cornucopias

of the sweetest treats,
until each has come to know
that sated, eternal sleep.
Such holy care not to disturb

tick or mealy worm or grub,
tread on dust or put out
even the merest life,
the way to light, O love!

Sister Mary Appassionata Addresses the
Marion County Writers' Guild

This voyeurism means you mortals
no sin, long as you try,
each heartstroke, to comprehend
your calling, this appalling apartness.

Only remember. When night beneath
constellations, streetlights, neon
inspires your lines, you can make out
the divine beauty of the mortal.

Perfect strangers, they'll hasten by,
faces blurred, eyes fathomless
as opals, hearts deep as the Blue Hole
of Castalia—forever, you could fall

through them. Tolling them
must be your duty, sacred and profane.
Know how little you count alone,
how close to God you grow by inventing

the proper, common name of everything,
fitting teeth and tongue to words
so lovingly each becomes a taste,
brackish as blood and just as sweet.

You'll learn the price of passion,
to grow even more quickly old,
visions burning holes in heart and soul,
even those who love you guarding

their secrets. There's no dark,
writers, you can't see into,

witnessing so ignites you, revisioning
the world until you get it right.

And everyone you care for lives forever.

Sister Mary Appassionata to the Human Awareness Class: Notes toward the Perfection of Sex

1.

Notker, sagest monk of St. Gall,
we praise as patron saint of water
because the duke of Bavaria, to try
the great physician, substituted

for his own a measure drawn
from an eight-month-pregnant woman.
Notker pretended prayerful study,
winked at the brothers, turned to the duke

and, raising the vial high, cried
Praise the Savior, Lord of Sex.
Within thirty days you'll be made
the instrument of a greater miracle

than the Virgin birth or Incarnation.
Call in chroniclers, goliards, jongleurs.
—And don't forget the midwives.
He was named at once the Ducal Physician.

So you see, to the good and cynical,
faith means the certainty that miracles
are born only in high deserts of doubt:
all at once water from the rock, tinkling.

2.

The trouble with Alcibiades?
Bion the Borysthenite tells us
that in his pretty youth he stole husbands
from their wives, and older, wives

from husbands — or was it the other way
around? No matter. It was the *stealing*

of the one and only gift that must be
freely given, gratefully taken,

perfectly shared, that cooked his goose.
Still today, made to go both ways

around Venus at light speed, many shades
too close to merciless light, he burns.

3.
Growing horny, Diogenes the cynic
would relieve himself in the marketplace,
mothers and children gaping, big-eyed,

as the stiff lover whooped and growled,
pricked by shards of uneternal urns
slick with rancid oil and wine,

rolling through rotting grape leaves
and fly-blown butcher's guts,
a great man dancing solo with his hand,

after which, panting, he'd sadly say,
*Would to heaven it were enough to rub
one's belly to quench one's hunger,*

scratch one's head to know it all.
Too truthful for his own good, he believed
that a lantern grasped in the hand

could point upward to honesty,
that love had to begin within the self
before it could be shared without.

4.
Aping Pliny, Francis de Sales railed
at his too-human flock for thinking small

when they thought of love:
Go to the elephant, thou sluggards.
It's their stupendous modesty.
They mate every three years, and then
it takes five days of labor
to find a way to mount
to trumpeting joy. Talk about
your foreplay. Here's generation
on the grandest scale. They remember
the deadly pitch and yaw
of the dance of Noah's heroic last two,
the need to share without crushing fore or aft
with the shifting cargo of passion's storms;
and they find a lovers' lane so far removed
that no human to this day has seen
their great act in the wild.

On the sixth day two lumbering lovebirds
return, and trot massively to the river
to give one another a shower bath,
too delicate to rejoin the herd unpurified.
Adultery's unheard of among elephants—
even in the show-biz circus world.
Say what you will about rabbits,
goats, birds and bees: you humans,
when you feel the strident need
to act like beasts together,
could do worse than this unforgetting
of the world's relentless gravity,
love's merciless, merciful weight,
and strive, like the elephant, to make it big.

5.
Wilhelm Reich, orgone master, you found
the antidote for hatred's poison, dance
of angels, only cure for what burns us up
through the mortal half-life of a life lived alone.

Satan, had he known, would've played it straight,
slithering down from that tree to urge on

naked Eve and Adam. Pharaoh would've had the sense
to let my people, as they pleased, come and go.

You showed us there's only one text to history:
the scorecard of who did it — or wanted to
do it more than anything else — to whom
and in how many ways. This fine, divine frenzy.

Your way, woman and man can mount to heaven,
go rigid as boneyard marble and be brought back
supple as a willow switch or river reed,
so new not even their own mothers know them.

Your rays shimmer August country macadam
where pairs of nighthawks, killdeer and vireos
swoop with fireflies through God's charged air
to fire every dawn and sunfall. Making the world.

Your static twinkles planets, novae and dwarfs
of a million myths, choreography of wind, wave,
menses and rut, immortal shivers up the spine,
the gasp of every writhing, striving twosome.

Love's utter whatness, hue of Elmo's holy fire,
borealis igniting aspen and pine, everybody bright
with Kirlian aura. You showed what miracles
we are, bushes ablaze yet never consumed.

It's a dead pelvis that keeps each neurotic
from knowing what's what, you taught us.
The cry and sighing of even the least
of earthly lovers becomes the song of songs.

V

On the Nature *of Symmetry*
from The Appassionata
Lectures

Sister Mary Appassionata Lectures the Anatomy
Class: Doctrines of the Nose

Upright now, we're two feet too high to smell
the ground, but it helps us find our way
through every wood, and even into love,
though it gets in the way of the simplest kiss.
A sign of what's below. Women who've lost
their ovaries have no sense of smell.
A man's nose will let you know how long he'll
last, a woman's will show how deep the well,
how high the moon. Joanna Queen of Naples
chose her partner by its breadth and heft.
England's Canute, sensitive as most rulers are
to the efficacy of symbol and sign,
punished adulterers, women and men, by hacking off
the nose. There was no hiding the wounds
of *this* circumcision. All the body's
softest tissue swells like buds in spring
when we're aroused. Too much love's a fever
and we can't breathe. Like the Shunemite's son
brought back from death by Elisha, when
we sneeze it means that while we're well on the way
to pyre, urn or grave, we've still a way to go.
When death comes near, it tries to rob us of all sense,
take our breath away, lead us by the nose.
We can't help but read its scents on every wind.

Sister Mary Appassionata to the Optometry Class: Doctrines of the Eye

I remember well the time when the thought of the eye made me cold all over.
  —Charles Darwin

1.
The Master Craftsman shapes each pair of eyes,
rolling them like balls of dough between hands
spinning fast as the potter's wheel. Some He makes
to focus on things of this world, myopia of wanting

what surrounds us, every other body, landscapes
we clutter with stuff. Others He fashions to
perceive what's distant, up to a universe away,
making seers who survey, foresighters, hindsighters.

Some He forgets to polish, thus some of us must
bear astigmatisms of heart and soul, hunting
pieces missing from the puzzle, black holes
disrupting perfect circles of His perfect light.

A few He makes opaque, to remind us of all there is
that can't be seen. Most He gets just right,
to make the near far and far near, our vision
the equilibrium of all that has been, will be, is.

2.
Only place the brain's laid bare, it's where
we're softest, yet its beams are laser-sharp,
enough to cut each seer out of the prison of skull,
parents' fearful cave. Beyond the body's wall

we're made to learn we're unimmortal. Just as we
breathe sighs of our least and greatest dead,
each Jane or John Doe and Leonardo, we see through their eyes.
We're never alone, always alone, eyes mean.

There can be no blind solipsism for good lookers.
Pupils grow huge in beauty's presence, contract at
what's sordid or spiteful. God put more rods, to feel
light, at retina's periphery, and more cones, to read

color, at the center. Thus the glimmer most far,
our hope, night's lovely chaos blossoming, we can know
only through the corner of the eye, truth of this life
told only slant, and what we ogle, ache openly for,

gaze longingly on, we see less well, color too bright.
Want a vision of the future? Close your eyes. For
the dream that redeems over and over, open them again
and for the briefest shining moment you've just been born.

Sister Mary Appassionata Lectures the Pre-Med Class: Doctrines of Sweat

In the sweat of thy face shalt thou eat bread,
till thou return unto the ground.
　—Genesis

Three million sweat glands
on every body keep it cool,
conduct each day's rising heat

like lightning rods to earth,
pores notched by God's bright awl
to make a sieve of each soul,

bailing out our bony, fleshy ark.
Time declines us like August cubes
until we're stiff and sere as

raisins, parchment, year-old jerky.
Any fight, fair or not, cold must
win. A doctor with a good nose

knows what we're dying for,
reads the sense of herpes, T.B.
and cholera, schizophrenia, fear

of one-too-many moments: each
writes its name on the nearest,
merest wind. Even love. In Rome

the god Conisalus regulated
the flow of perspiration to ease
the friction between every loving two.

It's the stain of generation,
its issue, essence, brackish as
the sea that brewed us, that we

slithered from stained with mud.
Distilled from pursuit of labor, joy,
our brief and desperate rain.

Sister Mary Appassionata to the Introductory Astronomy Class: Heartbeat and Mass, Every Last Breath

And God said, Let there be lights in the firmament
of the heaven to divide the day from the night;
and let them be for signs, and for seasons,
and for days and years.
    —Genesis

For every moment of light we win,
each beat of the heart in each heat
of the race, Old Sol sheds 4 million tons
of mass. In a mere 8 billion years

we'll be nothing but chunks of glacier
hurtling like manholes blown from sewers
through light years of limitless dark.
To live means bearing out these days

like candles through drafty mansions
while above us angry stars hiss like
garlic cloves in smoking olive oil,
souls racing down their wicks. Beyond

days and nights where can we be?
Each inhalation means we've won reprieve.
Each exhalation means the only sentence
long and short enough to fit the crime.

Sister Mary Appassionata Lectures the Eighth-Grade Boys and Girls on the Nature of Symmetry

No single life's symmetrical.
The Chinaman's right must ever be our left.
Earth spins right, we all lean
left. There's treachery on either side,
but what's left's easier to conceal.
Left testicle always hangs
lower. Right breast. God
places every heart a little
to the left; those who overlay the right thumb
with the left when they fold hands
to pray ask for too much passion, stumble
reasonless, lost in life's desert,
blizzard, woods, making a circle of hours
counterclockwise. They're nearly never
found. In sleep the flesh of the left side's
hotter, readier for love; the right's
more realistic. But turn around and each
becomes the other once again. God gave us
different hands so friends could clasp,
warriors war, lovers make a perfect fit;
so every other could become the rest of us
in every mirror.

Sister Mary Appassionata Lectures
the Biorhythm Class: Doctrines of Time

For though we slepe, or wake, or rome, or ryde,
Ay fleeth the tyme; it nyl no man abyde.
    —The Clerk's Tale

Stand a woman or man before the sun. The way
the shadow waxes and wanes means time and space,

prefigures ultimate night, a hole in light.
Most births arrive between midnight and dawn,

and most strokes, siren wail of life too new
or old, spring's ooze, winter's clutch and rime.

Oysters shipped from coast to coast in a vault
lightless as the tomb know when the moon's risen

over Midwest meadows and beds, open their mouths
to sing the beauty of the light. Mice offered

pneumonia at 4 A.M. never die. In a single life
we breathe 500 million times: 500 million prayers

to gods of capricious breeze. A single life means
50 tons of food, 41,645 liters of drink, then

each of us becomes incontinent in time. In
three weeks we can lose our skins to weather, wind,

chafing season, frictions of labor, love and hate.
The pineal gland, where Descartes put the soul,

ticks like a bedroom windup clock, governs
and alarms us with circadian rhythms of the spheres,

peristalsis, give and take of life and love,
the thrust, our *danse macabre.* How each night

cools the blood unless we love! We always
dream in ninety-minute scenes, souls going so erect

when we're aroused, limp when we can't bring ourselves
to love. Each worker forced to change shifts

goes a little mad, stewardesses bleed and bleed
when it's not time for them: variance and speed

mean all of us before we're ready grow a shade
too early or late to save ourselves. Night and day

are rooms we're born into, apartments that we rent,
our only inheritance, night and day the grave.

Sister Mary Appassionata to the Eighth-Grade
Boys and Girls: Doctrines of Divination

Alectryomancy: by cocks and hens, since
the best wisdom we can know resides
in the red head that twitches like
the dowser's hazel switch to point the way
to immortality, and because it's the layer
of the eggs who's wise enough to perfect
the art of love. *Bibliomancy:* by random
opening of The Book, because it's here
we've imprinted all character and heritage,
crazies, lovers and haters, believers, sayers,
wisdom of the tribes arrayed beneath us
page after page, tier upon tier, because
of which we stand so much taller.
Gastromancy: by rumbles coming from
the belly, because here we find the soul,
where earthly mixes with divine
in alchemist's retort to brew a life, what
we burn to be, to waste. *Lithomancy:*
by textures of stones, pillows and biers
of fallen kin, their last breaths all
our atmosphere, since these tell us what
we came from, the place where we
now dwell and where forever we're bound.
Sciomancy: by shapes and shades of shadow,
because if we know enough to read
the darkness all things made must cast,
we know that the universe, every child
of Eve and Adam, can be divided evenly
by light and night, and we know that
for everybody dwelling on this earth
time keeps running out.

Sister Mary Appassionata Lectures the Science
Class: Doctrines of the Elements

1.
God's a bag of wind, *primum mobile,* push come
to shove, motioner of stick, match, flint, elm-
shaker, hastener of spore, leaf, bee. All tides.

His first and best creation was the art of dark,
materia prima, background of our dreams, stuff
of love and lore, stage of each and every star,

but if He really were omnipotent He'd have made
the light before there was the dark, made us
good as we could be, made us last and last.

2.
The purest element? Fire, that in time consumes
what lives, greenest leafy oak burned to old man's
crabbed arthritic hand, pigweed smoking in the field,
sap bubbling from milkweed and wild onion, blood
from every heart and lung, marrow out of bone, hues
oozing fatally, steaming from the rose. Fire

makes us light enough to fly, borne on wind, to rise.
Earth's the heaviest element, worlds of life
arrayed by hand in layers of loam, enriched by flood,
fertility of silt that ages river into rill, that
shallows every harbor, dams each creek, clots
in artery and vein to blockade the heart. Earth's

what's heavy enough to fall. Burden we're made
to bear. Gravity of our lives. Air? Distilled from
flower, mountain and cloud, essence of mesa, noon
and tor, forest hill, time that blanches meadow so

it can rise again, shimmer of fen and field and road.
The gift of tongues. Song of every last breath.

Water's our brief sweet rain, made when earth
and fire make love, moving together and apart,
ancient dance through circles of burning, freezing
air. Water animates, informs semen and egg,
breast and uterus, lymph, tear and blood,
our bodies vessels shaped to hold God's love.

Sister Mary Appassionata Lectures
the Journalism Class: Doctrines of Belief

We carry within us the wonders we seek without.
  —Sir Thomas Browne

In each of us, where ancients thought the soul
was placed, closer to the heart than brain, we find
an issue of the *National Enquirer,* our every day
a tabloid page, our lips and fingers stained with cheap ink
of belief:

Fourteen Murdered by UFO. Bodies Drained of All Blood.

Housewife Lives in Hell. Scared to Death of Germs.

Ruins of Atlantis Discovered Beneath Lake Erie.

**Three Venusians Suspended in Liquid Nitrogen
at Wright-Patterson AFB.**

Ecuadorian Saint Performs Brain Surgery with Rusty Steak Knife.

Soviets Experimenting with Odorless, Tasteless Aphrodisiac.

Pope Reads Fatima Letter. Faints Dead Away.

Love Changes Michael Landon's Life.

Women and men wait behind shopping carts, metal frosting
white as flour from frozen food in plastic wrap, or
under hair dryers, time's desert heat ticking in their skulls.
They dream of camels galloping through needles' eyes,
wonderful plagues and catastrophes God rains on others,
sins of all to be read in each, following
the greatest commandment: *Thou Shalt Not Disbelieve.*

Sister Mary Appassionata Lectures the Parents
of the Eighth-Grade Boys and Girls

He'll harden the loan officer's heart, draw
around your neighborhood his thick red line, pit
management against labor at the gates of the plant.
He'll drive out good money with bad, dump steel

and color TVs on your markets, stain all ledgers
red as cheap wine and blood, the dim urban sun.
His awful breath will brew acid from the rain,
pit every statue, darken all your art. He'll put

Saturday night specials in the trembling hands
of lunatics and lovers. Herpes will increase
and multiply, chancres blossom on your flesh
like fat red flowers. Dogs in packs will bare

fangs at your children in vandalized playgrounds.
His frown will put out streetlights, blast plaster,
glass and brick, make your rivers run slow as sludge.
Vandal cells will riot up and down avenues

of the body, rats, bats and roaches inherit
every dwelling. He'll bless the arsonist's fire,
savor the stinking incense of the fruit of your decay.
Like dead limbs He'll break your tankers across

the knees of every ocean. His rumbling quakes
will shake the cores of your reactors. He'll
wrap your souls in barbed wire. His security lights
will drive you blind. He'll see to it that

the moment the children know they're bound to live
in the world you made, they'll realize they can't;
that the moment they realize the hell you made,
they'll know just why you have to die.

Sister Mary Appassionata Lectures the Eighth-Grade Boys and Girls: To Punish the Cities

He sends His dirtiest wind
to force the skirts of our women
over their faces, that violent men
may gaze upon their nakedness.

On lust's grindstone,
the strop of competition, He
hones the razors and knives we use
to still one another's hearts.

We hear His song in sirens,
grinding gears, groan
and fume of crowded summer buses,
a blue pall rising from each street

bitter enough to set the teeth
on edge, smite shin upon shin,
kindle an ache in every heart
and groin, drive us blind.

His angels? Larceny and Arson.
When we transgress, He doesn't turn
the other cheek. Who looks Him
in the eye becomes concrete.

Sister Mary Appassionata Lectures the Zoology Class: Doctrines of the Beast

Go to the ant, thou sluggard. Ants can't sleep
knowing the giant race of gods of blunder and caprice,
thunderers whose soles and heels mean sudden nothingness.
Where's room for unbelief beneath such abrupt tons

of danger dropping out of heaven? Such industry. Kill
one ant and its mourning tribe begins to dig your grave.
Besides the ant nine animals Mohammed admitted to paradise:
Al Borak, sun-white steed that galloped him all the way

to seventh heaven, because woman and man, conceived to be
just slow enough, spend their lives worshipping velocity,
sudden spark, love's light speed; Al Kaswa, the prophet's
favorite camel, since only those beasts who know no thirst

can be trusted as we go; Balaam's eloquent ass, because
through sure-footedness and plod this burdened beast
saw an angel even the prophet looked right through; Jonah's
whale, the ram Abraham traded to death for a son, the ox

of Moses and Noah's dove, and the cuckoo, since God
made animals to bear testimony to our body of weakness,
to eat our every sin, feasts we could tell time by;
also Katmir, dog who stood watch outside the cave of the sleepers

of Ephesus without food or sleep for 309 years. Beasts
mean a way to trust, believe and love. Consider the bee,
angels who fled the garden to bring us color, heaven's scents.
Their art now lights our nights and rites, their labor

blooming above each field, life's bright sweet love.

VI

Feeding the Dead
from The Appassionata
Doctrines

Sister Mary Appassionata Lectures
the Eighth-Grade Boys and Girls:
Every Day Another Snake

And God gave Adam hands, fingers
smooth enough to soothe, deft enough
to create, arms long enough to reach,
but Adam sinned by trying to please
himself alone, so God made Eve, and
to her too gave hands, fingers, arms,
but Eve sinned by wanting to please
herself before all else, so God was forced
to make the snake, but by this time
He'd learned a lesson, and made it
limbless, and its slither and hiss
made Adam work, and Eve, until
their hands grew rough as pumice,
fingers gnarled from scrabbling for roots
in rocky soil, sewing greasy skins
callous-tough with blunt bone needles,
arms bent from a winter's weight
of firewood, a spring field's
depth of stone and clay.

Still today women and men come
into the world with the means to soothe,
create and reach, but a burning lust
to please nobody else. Every day
God's forced to make another snake.

Sister Mary Appassionata Lectures
the Eighth-Grade Boys and Girls:
The Second Day

When He said on that first dark day
"Give me light," there flew in
from nothingness legions of creatures
plumaged in sunshine, each pair of wings
a song. He gave them names like *Basso*
and *Contralto, Wind-in-Pines* and *Lark*.
He spent the rest of the day listening.

But by the piercing dawn of the second day
the song fell apart, harmony wavering
and cracking, the heavens sounding like
a turntable with too many records piled on;
and He didn't care for the way some angels
sang to others, wings fluttering together,
on every cloud an act of brazen love.

So when He divided the waters under
the firmament from the waters above,
the angels whose feathers grew dim with sweat,
wet with wanting and coarse enough to touch
could no longer fly, and fell terribly
from the sky, screams fading as they dropped
through air and earth and into fire.

Thus were demons created, numbering,
the Talmud tells us, exactly 7,495,926,
though some believe each infant brings along
when he falls to earth another thousand.
This is how things got the way they are.
This second day alone of all the seven
of the week wasn't called "good."

Sister Mary Appassionata Lectures
the Eighth-Grade Boys and Girls:
The Family Jewels

In the beginning He put man's parts
of love where today you find the nose,
and woman's where her mouth is now.
But she grew too lean and hungry;
he couldn't stop sneezing. Loving,
they couldn't catch their breath.
Neither could get a word in edgewise.

So He put them where today you find
the hands, but it became too hard
to separate the gestures of friends
and lovers. An embrace came to mean
too little, a handshake much too much.
The tribes couldn't discern work from play,
war from peace, itch from scratch. So

He put the instruments of love where
they belong, mouth for ardor, zeal
and pleas, nose for scents, hands
to make or break, give and take, things
of passion closer to the heart than
brain, veiled as all great beauty
must be. Hidden from the greedy

and profane, the family jewels.

Sister Mary Appassionata Lectures
the Bible Study Class: Noah

Months and months adrift
and more marooned on a mountain
in a leaking, three-storied boat of gopher wood
filled with his family,
all clean animals by sevens, unclean
by twos, stench of beasts, mildew and pitch
a powerful perfume wafting to heaven,
incense of all flesh.

The first forty days they hated Him, hearing
beyond bellow and babble below
and rain on the roof loud as static
on a stormy night
the faint cries of those they floated by,
whose only sin was to be born
outside the covenant.
One by one the unbelievers lost their grip
or grew too faint to stroke and kick
and slipped back into the sea
all life once had crawled from,
lungs and fingers a useless evolution.

Then it stopped. Hate became fearing,
then vigilance and resolution. It was
the most precious cargo ever to float.
They had to love, and love again.
Hating could only mean another storm.
They were the world compressed to three hundred cubits
by fifty by thirty,
one jagged rock, tree or temple-top
from joining the bloated things
floating toward them and away
white as bone, as salt.

House of all seed, memory and gene,
every last word, there was nothing for them but
to practice being fruitful.

Even the beasts recognized the obligation,
screaming elephants plaiting trunk and tail
into lovers' knots, camels undulating
humps, rocking the boat
with their lumbering enthusiasm,
sparrow, dragonfly and crow,
nighthawk and finch in twos reckless
in air, rabbit, pig, goat and dog
glassy-eyed, love an essence, pulse, hunger,
every male rigid as death
minute by minute, females damp as April dew,
flopping about like trout out of water,
coming together for all they were worth,
dancing over the killing waves.

In those days, not to exceed
their parents' voyaging,
not to last just long enough, was to perish.
Learning to keep afloat
just above danger, like the dove in search of olives,
they taught us generation,
and that endurance always comes in pairs.

Sister Mary Appassionata Lectures
the Human Behavior Class:
One Mouth, Love and Ache

Because God put in one mouth
both tongue and teeth, each of us
must give and take both love and ache,
wear the masks of song and snarl,
learn how often words are made to break.

Sister Mary Appassionata Lectures
the Eighth-Grade Boys and Girls
on the Nature of the Candle

There are many instances during the Middle Ages of persons
having a candle made, as a special devotion, of the same
height or the same weight as themselves.
   —Curiosities of Popular Customs

It stands to reason. Wax crafted by bees,
tallow of vegetable or beast rendered just hard enough
to stand, to support the flame that dances
dangerously before the slightest breath, wick
running the body's length, spinal cord
that makes all parts a whole, intelligence
warming whatever comes near, touch of love,
to dispel the sentence of night after night,
only need to be, but eating a hole
in the center, faith consuming flesh from the inside,
running toward the heart, a fuse,
utter dark biding its time under the tongue,
inside each tooth and bone, life drowning
in the rising tide of life, deadly depth
of every day, price we're made to pay
for our season of light, last breath
a hiss or sigh as sun floods windows
to bear the soul away, what's left of us lying
gutted, guttered, cold, scents
of our brief wisdom lingering in the room.

Sister Mary Appassionata Lectures
the Science Class:
Fossils, Physics, Apple, Heart

Fossil bones, splintered bits of pelvis,
jawbone, tooth and skull aren't
of early apes and men
but of fallen angels made by greed too gross
to fly, who shattered when they hit the ground.

We know from physics every clock
winds down, each woman and man lies down
one more time than necessary for sleep or love.
Every movement culminates in stone,
each light and life in the ocean of night.

Drowned bodies, drunkards, heroes, saviors
surface always on the third day.

Virgin wool cures the deepest ache or burn.

Girls with big breasts and too much heart won't
fit into heaven. The boy who can unclasp
a girl's brassiere with one hand
knows too much for his own good
and all his life will have his hands full,
his mouth open at the wrong time.

The key to happiness? Knowing every second
of every day what to do with the hands,
when to loose or hold the tongue.

The holiest creatures are those that fly. God
Himself's part falcon, cuckoo, pelican, dove.

The girl who indulges herself
by climbing spiked fences, riding a horse

with too much passion, stooping too often
to pick mushroom or orchid
or dreaming of lovers who feel as she does
will from the wedding night on
be too easy on her husband.

Man's the only animal dumb enough to try
to cry back the dead, take
another's life only out of spite,
give his life for love.

Those whose eyebrows meet can never be trusted.

Women named Agnes always go mad.

No hunger justifies eating an apple
without first bringing it to life by breathing
on it, filling it with beauty
by rubbing it across the heart.

Sister Mary Appassionata Lectures
the Sex Education Class:
Doctrines of the Kiss

Behold the birds of the air, how
they bill and coo, the nuzzling
of beasts in each field, elephants
even, braiding lumbering trunks.
Observe cats licking kittens, dogs
how they sniff, baboons groom.

Homer, wise as he was, was blind
when it came time to kiss. Celts
could find no word for it.
Egyptians taught us how to inhale
at one another to unite two souls.
Eskimos, Maoris and Malays press

noses. One Yakut rubs another's
cheek with cold, cold lips, then
waits for inspiration. The French
sin with the tip of the tongue,
grow so hot together they lose
all sense of up or down. Babies

and lovers suckle and bite,
mothers and lovers peck, heal our
every wound. It's the way we set
our seal, make peace, betray
another's savior or mate, bring
ourselves luck, take leave of

our senses, comrades. When we
kiss, every sleeping beauty grows
aroused for dawn, each frog becomes
charming prince. The kiss

makes one of two, involves all ten
senses: savor and feel, love's

scents, whisper and tongue, look;
yet nothing we do, no gesture
makes us more ethereal, gets us
farther from the solitary hell of
bone. When we give our lips away
we're never more ourselves.

Sister Mary Appassionata Lectures
the Sex Education Class:
Historia sexualis

In every drop of semen are seven-times-seventy
angels, golden, man-warm and God-faced, who
use their wings to swim. Each egg
inside a woman bears a portrait of the Virgin.

To see where one so lovely came from, Nero
slit open his mother's belly,
made a shrine of her pelvis.

St. Peter appeared to Agatha in prison
just before she was torn apart
to return to her on a silver plate
the breasts she'd lost the night before
to a Roman and his stubby sword.

Who knows the size of a man's nose
knows the length and circumference of the art
that grows below.

When Adam lost his rib, he also lost
the hair that flourished on his palms.

If every act of passion together or alone
didn't cost a year of life,
women and men would live forever.
If you move together, as you were made to do,
you must wait for one another. At the instant
of sharpest joy a year of life's exchanged.
If you accept this gift before the one
you're with gets his or hers, you've sinned
the greatest sin and must, the moment strength
returns, begin to move again.

Sister Mary Appassionata Lectures
the Eighth-Grade Boys and Girls
on the Nature of Eloquence

German tribes hung the heads
of their most eloquent dead
in trees, where, open-mouthed,
they'd sing as long as bone
endured to the rhythms
of God's endless waltz, the wind.

Kleomenes of Sparta kept the head
of his most trusted friend Archonides
in a honey jar, to consult
in times of crisis, for when
things are most bitter,
no counsel's sweeter than that
of one who's loved beyond the grave.

The Irish mixed a fistful of brains
from a lost comrade with the earth
he shadowed and made bitter
by his fall, molding a weapon that,
when tempered by the fire and lament
of a long night's vigil, would live
again when flung, finding the murderer
by listening for his voice,
looking into his face, smart enough
to take a shattering revenge,
eloquent enough to shape a song
his sons would sing forever
after he fell back to dust and clay.

Sister Mary Appassionata Lectures
the Cinematography Class:
Late, Late Movie

During each black and white frame
of *It Came from Beneath the Sea,*
while lovers walk about in twos
or threes, climb stairs together,
lock and bolt their doors,
the ocean moans just behind or below,
hisses slowly up the beach where
they lie entwined, a brackish greed
seething weedy and shrill, a rage.

But the breathless truths of those
who've glimpsed the thing
about to slither and roar through
its rites ashore are thought
too passionate, mad. Waves
conquer the harbor in time. Scene
after scene, each actor becomes
an island. The sea screams to be
heard over rising violins, god

who's come back for his children.

Sister Mary Appassionata Lectures
the Creative Writing Class:
Naming Everything Again

And whatsoever Adam called every living creature, that was the name thereof.
  —Genesis

We're designated to travel
from a world where nothing needs
a name to this, where all things cry out
for one. *Cleveland, Ohio.*
Ascension of Our Lord Church.
Giovanni. John. Father.
Eastern Daylight Saving Time.
Undertaker.
Extreme Unction.
Heart.
Beat.
We're made to describe the way
from dark and silence to here,
through every letter, to learn that,
sure as night defines the day, to be
means naming everything again.

Sister Mary Appassionata Lectures
the Home Ec Class: The Feast

On time for every meal
whether I set them a place
or not, the family ghosts
assemble around the table.
My parents and theirs, dead

uncles, cousins and friends
light as steam, subtle as
anise, bay leaf or sage,
study me as I pierce and carve,
slice and chew, pause to savor.

Grease of flesh stains lips
and fingertips, coats teeth
and tongue as rust does iron
or dust the porcelain figurines
in the proper homes of

proper old ladies. Course
after course, meal after meal
and still they're unsatisfied.
Grandfather, speck of oregano
stuck between front teeth,

wipes sauce red as heart's blood
from his plate with a crust,
holds up a glass to ask for
more wine. "But you can't be
thirsty," I whisper. We're

destined to meet like this
three times each day, the family

become a rite, a thirst we'll
never slake, hunger ever
unappeased, our need, the feast.

Sister Mary Appassionata,
America's Adviser to the Lovelorn

Q.
My husband's heart's gone
fat and blind, heavy
as a side of beef twisting
slowly in an icy locker,
ham hocks and pork snouts
in the market's cooler, lungs
porous as torn cheesecloth,
two handfuls of greasy suet,
tongue rough as the bull's.

Where love once reared
its proud red head a lamprey
wriggles, limp as old garden hose.
There was a time he could blast
off its silver maple limb
a new brown squirrel
at two hundred yards. Now
he can't see a thing below his
belly. What do you advise?

A.
Every dream disobeyed
becomes by light of dawn
a wound, five pounds more
of ache: lungspot, heartclot,
stone stuck up duct, clogged glands,
chilled glans, handfuls
of vandal cells rioting through
a body's bourgeois avenues.
Heed the dreams, love, you'll

make him over again.
Saved by the all-too-human need
to sleep and dream at the same time,
you'll learn what to wear, where
to have the hole dug, how to
lower him away under stone in a spray
of holy water and tears, cut mums,
poppies, lilies, baby's breath.
In time all milk turns, meat goes bad.

Soon enough you'll be one again,
sweet and fresh, everlasting. Like death.

Sister Mary Appassionata Lectures
the History Class: Life of the Saint

All his life it hurt like
ice on a bad tooth to live
in the body: lungs gravel-loud,
throat scalding at each inclination,
bones kindling-brittle when he

misstepped or, trying to cast off
too soon, was yanked back to earth.
The toughening, savage heart arrhythmic,
each silence between beats
a premonition, always too fast or slow

for him to keep in step yet
not once overtaking desire.
The magic wand between the legs,
stately pine or limp garter snake
at the worst of times, its will

his own. He saw at once what
depth and breadth meant to the deer,
the sparrow and calf, the trout,
mouth snapping shut on the hurt
of its last supper. His parents

grew to hardened hearts, bags
of precious wind, bushels of teeth,
hair, bone, guilt and rings. Flesh
a target of every barbed hunger,
one more than it could elude at last,

the weight, darkness he was made to bear.

Sister Mary Appassionata Lectures
the Bible Study Class: Homage to Onan

Resurrection man, father
of the race and genocide,
puppeteer playing God,

you're empty gesture,
open hand a blessing, fist
a curse. As powerful

nearly as the one who
waits with finger on button
poised to end it all

with the biggest bang.
Impossible as the needle
through the camel's eye,

love born dying at your feet.
What's the sentence to fit
such crime? As part of

your passion, to endure
whenever alone desire's
shivering frictions until

you're worn out, to bear
the unbearable weight,
gravity of humanity, to

stumble down streets
thronged with lovers fit
for one another, those who

didn't fail, to move to death.

Sister Mary Appassionata Lectures
the Religion and Mythology Classes:
Frogs and Foreskins, Heart and Tongue

A frog from Egypt's plague, piece of reed
from baby Moses' yacht. Two lumps of lard—
what's left of Lawrence and Joan. A piece
of Shadrach's unsinged robe. Pine shavings
curlicued from Joseph's plane, sawdust
from his rasp, divine chips off
the old block. The Bambino's foreskin.
Feathers from Noah's dove, droppings from
the one that blessed the Apostles' tongues,
the raucous jay Francis shut up with his
simple singing. Feathers from
the engendering wings of Gabriel.
Wormy core of Adam's unswallowable apple.
Comb from the cock that crowed to reproach
Peter. Bones from Balaam's
eloquent ass. Feet of four and twenty crows
knocked out of the sky by Loreto's
high-flying house. Pickled in a canning jar:
Lucy's most discerning eyes, Agatha's nipples,
the herring bone Blaise made the boy cough up,
whole and unaltered hymens of Veronica
and Mary; Holofernes' ear, Cecilia's
vocal cords, heart and tongue of Isaac Jogues,
Abel's skull, irreparably shattered.
A quart of milk from Mary's right breast.

We can't be damned for not believing in these;
only for being so cocksure this world's
a place narrow as the space between our own
eyes and ears, death's-head cell of darkness and bone,
hell of thinking always only that we know.

Sister Mary Appassionata Lectures
the Clinical Psychology Class
on the Life and Death of
Blessed Eustochium of Padua

Most of the townsfolk who clumped
each night around the convent wall like
leukocytes around an infection
and demanded that she be shut up for good,
most thought her possessed
of too little morning, too much night.
Daughter of a nun who had no alms
to give a handsome beggar
and no qualms about giving herself instead,
she was always mother's little girl,
confusing give and take, in and out,
love and love. Her pious smiles adorned
the curses she recited each time some demon
slipped between her lips
to waltz and polka her around the floor.
She once was found alone in her cell
naked as Jesus in the manger, eyes
shut tight but smiling the smile
you don't get from dreaming.
The sisters, turning their faces to avoid
the devotion and despair wedded
in her eyes, tried to make her pure again
with the fire of the scourge. How such
holiness hurt her isn't recorded.
After death the embalmers read
with trembling fingers just below the breast
the scarred letters in a child's hand,
J E S U S. She's patroness of those
pulled apart by gravities of earth and sky,
all who're not themselves alone, emblem
of the darknesses that frame each day.

Sister Mary Appassionata Lectures
the Creative Writing Class:
The Evangelist

John, Zebedee's son, best writer
of the twelve, you made Him, then
with a critical eye watched Him
shiver and mope through the final supper,
learned His voice and hate for the state
so well you made them your own,

until years later, head nodding
with the fleeting certainties of age,
you filled a book with sixes and sevens,
locust and scorpion swarming over
sinners who winked at revelation,
giggled at anything you had to say.

Preaching to Rome's Senate
from your cauldron of bubbling oil,
finding yourself unable to die
with so many manuscripts unpublished,
you taught us writing justifies
doubt and loving, showed us

words are always our salvation.

Sister Mary Appassionata Lectures
the Theology Class
on the Life and Death of St. Teresa

She's become a journey.

Her left arm's at Lisbon,
fingers of the right hand at Seville, Avila, Paris,
Brussels, Rome.
Right foot in Rome, a slice of flesh.
One tooth in Venice.
Piacenza boasts of a napkin stained with her blood.
Milan keeps a piece of the heart, another tooth.
Lump of her flesh in Naples, scapular.
Her slippers at Avila,
most of the torso at Alva,
at Cagliari her veil.
The wooden cross she used to beat the demons
sent to try her, at Rome. Also Brussels.
Two very large slices of flesh in Krakow.

She lived to keep herself intact.
At the instant of death love tore her to pieces.

Sister Mary Appassionata Lectures
the Creative Writing Class:
Life of the Poet; or, the Storm

She spent that night shivering
the storm away in the enormity
of her bed, hands clenched
between legs, carried away by dream.

He looked like Jesus, face contorted
by passion and thorn. He smelled
of gin. He carried something
like a tree, one end scraping

a furrow in the dusty street.
His sandals slapped the soles
of his feet as he walked. She
followed, two steps to every one

of his, but gained no ground.
A hot wind hit her like a horrible idea.
She swelled at bodice and hip. "My
little girl," he said, but her profile

gave her away. He put something
against her, took her breath away.
So suddenly she was all woman. What
hurt her so when she awoke was that

nothing had changed. Every night
since, she wakes at least once to
the roaring of heartbeats, blood, bed
quaking with thunder, fighting for air

in a room loud with winds of words,
the storm consuming her outside and in.

Sister Mary Appassionata Proves to the Entomology Class that Woman and Man Descended from the Cricket

Our mothers and fathers,
sojourners in bogs, architects
of prairie clods, perennials
strewn over mountainsides,
forders of roiling creeks, herds,
loving under thatch and star,
each word together a bellows
heartening the flame, sang
to summer rain and generation,
feared only the sudden shrill bird
of fire or wind. Where they fell
cities were raised. We lost our ear
to concrete and brick, thick rivers
stagnant under iron spans, tug
and barge contending with siren,
horn, raucous hell of press, mill,
forge. Tonight just beyond
the bedroom wall our parents and the wind
will return to soothe earth's
August fever with a cool hand,
remind us of love's sympathetic magic,
leaping and creaking from clump
and bush, thick weedy field,
chanting the history of the world.

Sister Mary Appassionata Lectures
the Theology Class
on the Resourcefulness of Demons

When it's time for study,
they hang on my eyelids,
remind me of Chablis's
sweet French kiss, make the window
a shade too enthralling. They
take up residence under the tongue,
and when I most need to be
an inspiration, I'm made
to stutter, hem and haw. One
sits between my legs, and when
I'm in the middle of abstinence
and beauty strides into the room
on muscled thighs, imposing
itself between decades of the rosary,
makes outrageous demands, upsetting
the fragile balance I've
struggled to erect. In the library
they turn pages dark
with the laughter of lark and jay,
tittering of children
in the garden that's summer, bark
and whine of distant dogs. Much as we do,
a demon's what we leave undone. Far
as we go, a demon lies an inch
beyond, taunting. I know
where they've been by the wrinkles and creases
of a hot night's sleep, by what's left
in the bathwater when I rise steaming and clean.

Sister Mary Appassionata Recounts
a Folktale

No, no, no, no she said, squirming
beneath the convertible top
of the '57 Chevy, hemmed in
by his more experienced words,
defter hands. Out in the night
the brooding, drooling one-handed
danger the radio said had just escaped
stalked them both, but he was breathing
too loud for her to hear. *I'm*
saving myself. Take your hands
away. Take me home now please.
He did, the ache of teenage love denied
nearly doubling him over the wheel
each time he had to clutch or brake.
They found her father robed on his lawn,
hands on hips like some angry god,
enraged over rainbow bruises
on his little girl's throat,
the wrinkled skirt and angora sweater,
stains of mortal passion on his pants
and, just above where she sat, stuck
in the car's rag top, time's
glittering awful weapon lovely and lethal
as a scythe, the hook.

Sister Mary Appassionata Lectures
the Folklore Class:
Doctrines of the Strawberry

Mary, full of the mercy only
mothers know, hides the souls
of unchristened infants, guilty
as sure as they're born, in seeds
of strawberries, Jesus' favorite fruit,
and when He's picked and had His fill,
walking out into heaven's
misty meadows and groves weeping over
the gross appetites of the wicked,
thinness of the good, and after
nature's run its course, their beauty
passing through Him like too much
of any good thing, the seeds are left
to be covered with the dirt of paradise,
time's never ceasing tide, but soon
to rise again in blossoms of white flower
and plump red fruit, bitter and sweet
as blood, as life,
waiting for Him to come again.

Sister Mary Appassionata Lectures
the Eighth-Grade Boys and Girls
on the Things of This World,
the Things of the Other

1.
God's at the bottom of the Sea of Japan,
a giant catfish old as darkness, slumbering
in fecund ooze, compost of creation, slimy
as liver. He dreams the world. Each twitch

of His whiskers, fins and tail means
another city leveled, another ten thousand
in over their heads. Civilizations go
to sleep each night praying God won't stir

or flop, make waves; won't, raging, rise.

2.
In every sudden winter river, God's what
hardens, that beast and man might stiffly
walk or glide across, a miracle,
each exhalation an aura, halo of holiness.

God's what sizzles the frying egg from clear
to white, garlic's spinning hiss, blight
that hastens falling fruit, earth's kiss dark
as a bruise, awful hardness that seizes

every lover, corpse, His sticky seed our dew.

3.
The Pharaoh's personal physician was called
Shepherd of the Royal Anus, which goes
to show that sometimes gods move in
the commonest ways, words made flesh. Jesus

spat at blind men just to make them see.

4.

Rue cures the horniest witch's curse,
shrivels the lecher's stiff and massive passion.
Weasels and priests feed on its leaves
before going out to charm the snake.

Exorcists steep a leaf in blessed water

to tempt young girls from toadstools, scald
the throat of one possessed, sealing
the demon's blaspheming lips. In times of dread,
piles of smoldering dead, place it in church,

the baby's bed, near every mirror, fire,

it clears the head. Girls, put it where
your latest lover was, to draw out the ache
of generation. Life's a loss. Spend each day
adding, subtracting, recounting the expulsion

from the garden. Brew a cup of tears. And rue.

5.

The eyes shoot rays that photograph the world, no matter
how bad the composition, the light. Pius IX, good
and well-meaning as they come, had the evil eye. He once
looked a baby out of its mother's arms high above Rome's
cobblestones and watched it plummet to earth, a fat,
ripe melon. When he blessed, walls went out of plumb,
mortar was changed back to water and sand, laborers fell
screaming from heaven, scaffolding collapsing like
cards. Ships and virgins went down like tons
of bricks. Only a greater gift can guard against
the evil eye. Mussolini kept his hands in his pants pockets
when Alphonso of Spain came to see him. He knew a handful
of the family jewels can soothe the wound of sight,
overcome the most glittering malice. If in the last six months
you've shed no tear, God will fill your eyes with cataracts.
Still today we veil widows and brides, spend our hard-earned
coins on the eyes of the dead. My own father died

of a broken heart because his mother stared at a picture
of the Sacred Heart on the bedroom wall as her husband labored
above her to plant the seed, her cries of love a prayer.
Because of the eyes everything connects.

6.
Love equals gravity. A net. Handful of ocean
your mother carried in her belly, and with
your father warmed over hearth's glowing coals

to brew you. You kicked, swam, grew fins

and tail, feet, visage and soul: love's phylogeny.
Mother's fingers, woven behind your skull
fragile as an egg, held you as she sang you awake.
Each word caught. Your lovers' sure hands
will unravel the web to spin you new. It all

gives way the day you fall all the way to age.

Sister Mary Appassionata Lectures
the Pre-Med Class

I. A LESSON IN ANATOMY
Five hundred million years ago Mother Eve
suffered a terrible blow from God's
left hand. The top of her spinal cord,
wriggling like a snake, swelled
into a brain the size of two apples.

The vagus nerve ties head to heart,
body to soul. The brain makes us
both angel and beast, cynic and believer,
its tortuous corridors are endless, tubing
to cool the furnace of the heart.

The body's a vertebrate, its skin
and sinew dressing barest bone, but
the head's a crustacean, bony shell
encompassing memory, idea and will,
sweet meat that lies inside, making us

wise as the sea. Without memory we'd
read the same story every day, never
chilling our pleasure by seeing
the beginning with the last things
in mind, love the very same lover

over and over the first time, wake
each dawn wonderful and eloquent as Adam.
The splintered teeth and shins of saints
endear them to us. Charred timbers
of the ancient room we were born into,

bones are most enduring.

2. FIGURES OF LOVE, SPENDING OUR LIVES

Each cell's the image and likeness
of the wriggling, snake-tailed Adam
and the apple-sweet blood-plump egg
of Eve who came together in a garden
of their love the day it all began.

An act of love plugs in the universe
again, strews eels, oysters and salmon
under the seas, toadstools and lilies,
rams and ewes over fields, portraits
of two parents on every bedroom's wall.

Onan the Canaanite? What a waste.
The figures of love are counted always
in twos, above and below, behind
or in front, recto, verso, in and out.
Love's the one heat of every race,

lover and beloved against the clock.
The Flood rose over us because it grew
too easy for women and men to love
themselves. Cursed be they who spend
their lives in puddles on the ground.

3. THE FOUR FLUIDS

Chemistry informs us, quickens even
the dead. Four fluids God gave Adam
combine and recombine, gurgle
and roar, simmer and cool even as we do,
in the body's labyrinthine tubes.

Blood. Dark as well water when it
pools, deep enough to drown us all.
A race's history smeared thin as dust
over the pathologist's slide, life
inscribed, unfathomable as the tides.

Milk. Blood filtered by the loveliness
of breasts, kiss of aching nipples soft as

baby's breath, one of love's recurring
wounds, smooth as the belly rounded
and taut. In a frigid world, it's fire.

Tears. Blood conducted through canals
of sense: touch, sight, scents, listen
and sing. Juice fermented from fruit
of generation. It's how we pronounce
our sentence, mourn the receding sea.

Semen. Blood boiled, concentrated in
love's retort. Man's acrid dew. God's
manna brightening our fields even as we
sleep and love, live and breathe. Yeast
we rise by. Puddles of the sea that spawned us.

4. DOCTRINES OF THE BREATH
Long as we live we just can't overtake
the heart, which, even when it's resting,
strokes four times faster than the lungs.

Life culminates in exhalation. The last one
bears the soul, which flies out whistling
like a dove to search for solid ground.

He's a fool who, all ears, spends his life
listening, knowing every breath could be
the last. Only to listen means too much

gets by. Shamans breathe so fast they learn
to fly and see all things. Slow respiration
means no passion. The deepest meditation, only

time we reach the peace each of us seeks,
a place of hibernation cold as bone or snow,
only time we're really holy, means

no breath at all.

5. BACTERIA AND WEATHER, TREASURE AND BONES
Our dead we give back to bacteria,
beetle, grub and worm, who carry them
back to the elements, earth, water,
fire and air, where they're born again
into feather and snail, desert flower,
moss and star-dew, mildew, fog and wind.

Their softest breathing becomes all
our weather. Their burrows and barrows
are our valleys, their mounds our hills.
Rivers carry them back to us, away.
What we build they bear the weight of.
Every well and foundation we dig

reapportions the treasure of their bones.

6. THE NATURE OF LOVE
Because God couldn't figure how to be
everywhere, He invented mothers. Women and men

are the only animals that drink when there's no
thirst, love in and out of season, recognize
the lineaments of God beneath a lover's clothes.
God made us pupils, gave us rods and cones so we

could really see. Billions have gone, millions
today are on the way because they can't know. Love.

The paramecium, which needs no other to work
its history, still seeks out others like
itself, powerless to couple yet groping, clumping
through life's utter night toward love. Every fossil

solves for us part of love's puzzle, stones
and bones that bore us all the way from sea and tree

to now. Lovers wind like strands of protein,
dance of the double helix, Eve and Adam every time

again. It wounds and heals, drum of heart's systole
and diastole, urgent peristalsis of flesh and soul.

7. THE NATURE OF VISION
Look at a woman in that certain way
and you've already known her. (It was
a son looked on as a god who first saw

this.) Too much selfishness can drive
the young or old man blind, his eyes
clenched tightly as a fist. Because

we would not see, God grew mad enough
to spit, changed our dust to mud,
rubbed it on our eyes. Leonardo

saw that the artist's vision could
light the world. Hume showed us
we could look our Maker right in the eye.

No one's as wise or eloquent as the eye.
It knows 7 million colors, every
variation of night and day. We've only

so many words. Every feature of the heart's
terrain grows visible to one whose
shortsightedness has been corrected for by

love. Fleeting omens of our incipient blindness,
every sneeze chills, stills the heart, on
every pair of eyes calls down the dark.

Age? The blossoming astigmatism, last
great cataract, evening racing over fields,
sea beneath the storm, the starless night.

8. LAST THINGS
In the graveyard late at night, ear
to the ground, you can hear the dead

squeal, grunt like boar and sow, crackle
like fat dripping from the roasting spit

of time, burst like May seedpods,
speak your name in a parent's voice.
Most men slip into earth's hard sea
whispering their mother's name, most women,

their father's. In death a woman bleeds
under each horned moon, a man stays hard
as on the wedding night, both of them
sweating as if in fever or love.

In three years the coffin explodes
from all the nails and hair, every body's
progeny. Death will come at you
like no other lover, whipping your face

with her long hair as she rides you
away, man, bony thighs gripping you
hard, her voice a storm tormenting
the pine-tops, plunging his icy hand

between your limbs, woman, teeth and tongue
lightly at your throat, whispering "It's never
felt this way before." Death's got
many lovers, no friends but the crow and fly.

Some soils keep you plump and firm
forever, others suck you dry in just one day.
The higher the clouds, the better you weather;
the deeper the grave, the better you keep.

Sister Mary Appassionata Lectures
the Neurology Class

If woman and man are willful, mindful hunks
of tissue, blood and bone, what is it wills, minds

them? If they're wills and minds embodied to make them
real enough to move to love, what is it embodies them?

For two years Soviet scientists with stainless blades
sliced up Lenin's brain, yet learned nothing about

learning. Technicians splattered Walt Whitman's
brain on the laboratory floor and tried to claim

it was an accident. Is knowledge the last supper?
Worms learn tricks by feasting on worms who've already

learned. So do we cannibalize our past. The flash
of light erupting in the neural cell bright as

Venus rising or stars falling from heaven rescues us
from caves of skull, root and bark of limbs, blazes

into thought, a gift of fire, we think, we know.

Sister Mary Appassionata
to the Paleontology Class:
Before the Invention of Bone

It was 510 million years ago today
that scales of calcium phosphate
blossomed on fish. Before that,
grackles and songbirds, doves and hawks
hung limp as snakes from branches,
masses of entrails that obese priests
would unreel on eves of anything proposed,
erection, election, migration, pilgrimage.
Auguries all the same: *I wouldn't*
if I were you. It doesn't look good.
Odds are against it. Not your day.
Beware, beware. There was no question
of music, no matter what the wind,
no lust to try next horizons,
grass that was greener,
only standing pat in slough and mire,
admiring finite seas from each shore.
Sooner or later all beings
went an ounce too far and collapsed,
imploding to blobs of rag and gore,
puddles of fatality. Each body
meant tent without pole, temple
of Solomon without Hiram's timber,
oak lacking bole. And in the end
death left nothing to remind,
to be polished and worked
into timeless art, next to flesh
what we hold most dear, our heritage,
this obdurate life of bone.

Sister Mary Appassionata
to the Music Theory Class

In ancient France

growers would crucify
a large starling

in the midst of their vines
to startle away
several acres

of its ravenous tribe
with a great death-cry.

Not every note

of every song must call on
urgent imperatives

of territory, lust
just to beget.
All songs are sad.

Like mute swans,
when we sing,

if we care to be true,
we must cry nothing less
than our own death,

whistle of the last breath,
screeching of each nail,
stillness of all starlings.

Sister Mary Appassionata Lectures
the Bible as Lit Class:
Meditations on the Life of Noah

1.
Along the Ganges and Indus
it was Manu, between Eden's

Tigris and Euphrates it was
pious King Ziusudra, later

Utnapishtim, teacher of Gilgamesh,
all of whom, like our Noah,

were made to mean forever
because someone had to

invent boats and tales
once we lost our gills and fins.

2.
Legends say the ark had three decks,
lowest for animals, middle for
birds, topmost for humans, in twos

of course, but sexes kept separate
for there was penance going on,
woman's place and man's divided

by gargantuan corpses of Eve and Adam,
and still today we assign
our children rooms by myth, one parent

apart, above all beasts though we
think too well to be as good, above
even birds though we soon forget

the one song that tells us who
we are, able only in wildest dreams
to believe bone and guts can fly.

3.
Noah invented craft, the art to take
measurements exact enough to make
a near-perfect fit, courage

to take no stock in the braying
of unbelieving neighbors, patience
to wait out the worst heaven could let fall.

To him there was something wonderful
in trees, in earth's beastly stench,
a symphony in wings of flies, doves.

Heaven's spite had to dry, he knew.
He rediscovered nakedness, madness
of too much wine, invented the son's

laughing scorn. When he died he went
astonished, his tools proving useless,
age the flood there was no ark for.

Sister Mary Appassionata
to the Women's Studies Class:
An Angel Thrusts a Spear into
the Heart of St. Teresa of Avila

After the death of St. Teresa her heart was found to bear a long and deep mark.
    —Butler's Lives of the Saints
Je suis d'accord . . . que sainte Thérèse est bien morte d'un transport d'amour.
    —Dr. Jean Llermitte

Born outside the garden on the border
between too much heat and cold, conceived
as some of us are as the dream of two dreamers,
she was no stranger to angels or desire.
But this one was hard enough to make her
cry: muscle and sinew, hands rough as
any father's, knees as sharp. Not one
of Fra Lippi's urchins mugging for the artist,
wings jutting ludicrously from shoulder blades,
or Raphael's precious pudgy babies. This one
had business to carry out. He came
out of the dark, every saint's heaven and hell,
the shape and shade of holy. At first
she thought to hold him off with words.
She asked to be anyone, anywhere else.
His face flared up like a kitchen match
at midnight. In his left hand he hefted
the spear, its tip burning like shame.
Again and again he hit her heart hard,
hurting like nothing before. No
indifferent beak, heaving bull meat, no
gold shower, but close enough. His heat
was understanding. It filled her. What
earned her such burning? A gift
for recognizing all that can be without being
seen. What remains? The tombstone row
of years leading to dust, fistful
of ash and char, a life memoryless yet

unforgotten, composed of columns of type
in so many books, stilled, scarred heart's
eternal echo, utter nothing of love.

Sister Mary Appassionata Lectures
the Eighth-Grade Boys and Girls:
A Concise History of Witchcraft

For rebellion is as the sin of witchcraft, and stubbornness is as iniquity and idolatry.
  —1 Samuel

1.

The accused were stripped and bound and whipped
severely, then shaved and examined for the devil's
fingerprints. The instruments of torture
were blessed thoroughly by a priest—so often
hurt's administered and performed as a rite. Next
the victims underwent *strappado, squassation,*

thumbscrews, leg vises, Spanish boots, choking pear
and roasting chair, smoldering, sulfurous feathers
applied to underarms and groin, forced feeding
of herring soaked in brine with denial
of water, baths of slush and smoking oil, gouging
of eyes, ripping out of nails, teeth and hair,

hacking off of privates and nose, splintering
of toes, while judges interrogated them and scribes
painstakingly recorded each reply. This shows
that mankind has always been obsessed with asking
all the wrong questions, knowing all it needs
to know of religion and anatomy and tools,

writing and the law, nothing about love itself.

2.

Artificial insemination? Nothing new. For ages
succubi have drawn out semen from the man who
too much loves himself, and incubi have poured it
into the slumbering womb of the woman who wants
nobody else. Thus, like the gods themselves,

a woman and man may be virgins and at the same time
mothers and fathers, technically. And always
mothers and fathers prove themselves by the lives
of their daughters and sons to be either
angels or demons, merely human or divine.

3.
We're meant in everything we do to keep it
clean, of course, but it's *ritual* that's next to
godliness. St. Gregory tells us how a devil
entered a nun as she was eating lettuce. She'd

washed the lettuce and her hands, but forgot
to cross herself, to be reminded of the loss
of life it takes to make us live,
fathers, sons and holy ghosts, virgins, mothers,

the myths and deaths it takes to animate us.

4.
Nine knots govern potency, Virgil writes.
Witches know how to tie and untie the strands
of what we are, double helices of generation.
When a man becomes too soft to love, a woman
too high and dry, narrow and tight, when one of two

becomes too suddenly unlovely in the other's
sight, it means a witch at midnight in front of
a dying fire has tied and knotted a leather strip.
The ligature remains until the knots are found
and loosened. Fifty ways there are to tie

the knots, to diminish urination, copulation,
procreation. If you know no sorcery, just
have patience. Time too hates, and can tie knots
to weaken the force of every stream, dam
the flow, wither the heart's bouquet, make

a potter's field of every meadow, a desert of each bed.

Sister Mary Appassionata Lectures
the Studio Art Class:
Doctrines of Nakedness

1.

In Greece each cynic trotted about caked in mud,
lifting leg like bitch and pit bull, believing only
what could be mounted, perceived, taking on in time
the hue and shade of grave. Apollo's healing rite
meant nude virgin administering balm to nude patient,
proving art can make us whole. The Israelites
lost their shirts to the gold calf, and David lost
wife and kingdom to earn the right to sing unmuffled.
One disciple ran naked into night because of Judas's kiss.
The Iroquois paired off to dance uncovered together
to bring down on field and forest the sweat of the spirit.
To lovers and mirrors going bare's the loveliest wisdom.

2.

Even Luther undressed to scare off
temptation. There are times
when this earth's so cold
even a lightning god must be
wrapped in swaddling clothes
until death casts lots for
his seamless garment. Thus
still today in graveyards
we drape our angels in folds
of stony white even though,
like Adam, Eve and us, they
haven't a thing to hide.

3.

The Middle Ages knew four ways of human revelation.
Nuditas naturalis meant Eve and Adam before they went
down, babes, morons and savages who couldn't comprehend
the lies in which women and men try to cloak themselves.

Nuditas temporalis, nakedness of each of us before
chance and law, rattling bones of poverty, fate,
snake-eyes of age. *Nuditas virtualis* signified
the clarity of the seer, unadorned truths of the good,
anchorites, dendrites, pillar-sitters embracing God.
Nuditas criminalis was the sin of sins, hot lovers
bearing passion before all else, flaming sword
and molten sheath, hell of knowing our mortality too well.

From Exile, Sister Mary Appassionata
Writes to the Creative Writing Class

Any one of these three things
will make you close to God:

a sickness so hot and loud
your mouth can't spit or pray,

can't make excuses, forgets
the usual things to say; a flight

across a distant border to a land
where music's spoken and wonder's

the rule, where you need to look up
everything before you say a word;

a place to rest six feet deep, just
your size, dug with hands you've

made holy by teaching them work,
all your life to help you find the way

to care for and say, gesture and sign
of kindness, craft, every right word.

Sister Mary Appassionata Lectures
the Creative Writing Workshop:
This Dance

This witless spasm, wince or shiver,
an act natural as birth, gasp, rigor,

dangerous as the nocturnal migration
of songbirds, lark's trill circling stars;

this coma, the computer stuck fast
in an endless GOTO loop, no way to save

our labor but to crash; reckless flight
of the passion-addict too deep into lands

of ego ever to get back, heart and mind
held in every other's deadly grasp tight

as the Gila monster's jaws, shaman-trance
of pure madness: in fits and starts,

loop and whorl through every page's
wilderness, this dancing of the hand.

Sister Mary Appassionata Lectures
the Health Class:
To Keep the Blood from Running Cold

You'll need a lover with warm hands,
with other things to do but the desire
to stay, with the belief there's nowhere
holier than the space your body takes.
Enough salt and spice for the most jaded palate.
A little too much wine. Some great fear
rumbling like empty boxcars up and down
your spine, echoing from skull walls
like trash-can lids, screaming through
rooms of your heart like cats driven mad
by night and love. One or more young ones
in your image and likeness whose eyes
grow brighter the murkier yours turn,
who rise blazing each dawn as in
each morning mirror you shrivel and burn.
An enemy who goes to bed yearning,
unloved and alone, who prays to God
to chafe and chill you with the winds
he's known. A God who doesn't listen.

Sister Mary Appassionata Lectures
the Forestry Class:
Doctrines of the Fir

Hewn and hollowed out, it galloped
through faults in Troy's complacent walls.
Hallowed, it upheld in Solomon's temple
the weight of a mountain god's blustering.

Also heaven's revenge: a fir tree
split by lightning reminds us
of death's flashing hatchet
of the days our parents were cut down.

Only try to survive, it signifies.
Seeds of a cone grown straight up
ensure success in any endeavor,
gamble, toil, gambol, pleasure.

Sister to the death-yew, it's filled
with light to celebrate, each year's close,
love's bright heights and birth's shining,
the innocence of all things young.

Sister Mary Appassionata Explains
to the Classics Class Why So Many
of the Great Lovers, Heroes
and Saints Were Shepherds

Standing watch against the very dark, flock
stinking, bleating below while above it all
the head bursts with light, vast dance of planets,

harmonies of stars. Out of nowhere thrash and snarl
of assassin and prey, blood's ineradicable cry
gushing from matted wool, gathering in pools deep

as fear. Winters too cold for feeling, breath
becoming art before one's eyes, life a fire
of imagining, perfect lovers, God's reedy tenor.

August nights where the greatest torment means
to be clothed, rain hissing names of the body's
godlike parts, nothing to pattern breath upon but wind,

nothing to believe but seasons, night and dawn.

Sister Mary Appassionata Responds
to Questions from the Floor

Q.
Can God make a stone so heavy
He can't lift it?

A.
Yes and no.

Q.
If God knows the future,
how can anyone have free will?

A.
I'm not at liberty to say.

Q.
What's an eternity?

A.
We haven't the time
to go into that.

Q.
Why did God make us?

A.
Looking and hearing,
tasting and smelling, touching
to wonder. To do what we're
born for, love, to question.

Sister Mary Appassionata Lectures
the Social Behavior Class:
Friends, Those Who Love

Friends assemble to converse,
recall, chant litanies of doing,
having done, perhaps someday.
Friends must share, are just to compare,

while those who love must too soon
come to ache, measure life in strokes
on strop, whir of grindstone, consuming
by frictions, breath-song, tongue,

morning the final glassy stare,
and know in every separation the demon
of ice and bone who means them
darkness, sleeps beside them

all the way to dawn, shadows them
on either side of noon, whispering
There's nothing beyond flesh and blood
but nothing. Living only as they dream,

lovers are to mourn.

Sister Mary Appassionata Lectures
the Natural History Class:
Love and Curse, the Wind, the Words

Jesus rained on the dust his Father
made us of to brew a healing love

to teach us how to see, spat on ledgers
of the businessmen trading in the temple.

It's the sign to change our luck
or extinguish the glitter of the evil eye.

We wet the hook to lure the catch,
the hands to fit them to our work

or save them from the flames, fingertips
to learn the truth about all wealth.

It's the way to soothe any wound, sting
or burn of love too artless or old,

to show us where the wind's been before
it comes to drop us in our tracks, a blessing

to move us on, rain that sings us underground,
that makes the words of life again.

Sister Mary Appassionata
to the Bible in Translation Class:
Rites of Purification

To turn every light back on
in the house where someone
of your own tribe by his own hand
grew heavy enough with despair
to fall through his shadow, to cleanse

the hands you used in loving one
who felt loving you was but an act
or rite, brew over a fire on which
a shadow's never fallen the water
of purification squeezed from

the fat of a heifer without spot
who's known no yoke, blood of
parturition, spit and sweat
of an honest day's work, tears of love
old and brackish as the primal sea.

Stand in sun to make your shadow
do all that you do. Bathe the parts
lost to selfishness, scour the stain
of hurting others. You and shadow,
dance the sin away; drink what's left.

Remember: like cures like. Hurt
and curse can be purged only
by the flood of remembering, rite of
keeping alive the spirit of every dead,
the holy wind of every kind word.

Sister Mary Appassionata Speaks
during the Retreat of the Eighth-Grade
Boys and Girls

Three entrances to the world of fire:
slip of zipper; blouse gaping too wide
or at the wrong time; the mouth, lips,
tongue wagging with the latest passion.

You don't believe in flesh's urgencies?
Hold your hand two inches above the candle's
tear-shaped flame, or place your lips
on a sighing lover's flushed throat, then
tell me beauty doesn't move you, art,

blood, bone and skin don't matter.
Lot's daughters were forced to take the law
into their own hands. Potiphar's wife
spent her nights wrestling a eunuch.

For what she did, who are we to blame her?
Dominic Savio and Teresa tried to stay saints
by forcing their eyes away from loveliness,
crying to put out every fire. They only
gave themselves headaches. Even the Savior

had an eye for beauty. The young lovers
found the morning after twined in sin,
rigid and blue with nature's last rapture,
eyes glassy with passion, the exhaust

of the '57 Chevy clogged with snow
in the drift they'd backed into in their haste
to age, clothes thrown around the backseat
like crumpled Christmas wrapping? They
lost their minds, perhaps, and we their names,

but the goodness they gave to one another,
dexterities of love, the fire they made
by moving limbs together, long as together
we live and breathe, never will grow cold.

Sister Mary Appassionata
Addresses the V.F.W.

And the land cannot be cleansed of blood that is shed therein,
but by the blood of him that shed it.
    —Numbers

The madness of the blood! Only blood
erases its own signature, only more,

drop subsumed by handful, as forest crowds
inundate each man-shaped ash or pine,

the ounce irreclaimable in the pool,
until through streets of Saigon, Teheran,

Belfast and Beirut a torrent bears away
your door, every neighbor, stains

children of rich and poor, lover's
bed and nursery floor, gushes from between

thighs of swollen wailing wives, wounds
blooming on flesh of gods and men

made breathless by hate's perfect stench,
the tongue severed, an artless stub,

until in time like fragile arteries around
every naked liver, spleen and heart

every river running to the sea runs red.

Sister Mary Appassionata Lectures
the Architecture Class:
Doctrines of the Wall

For the stone shall cry out of the wall and the beam out of the timber shall answer it.
  —Habakkuk

In the city where sons come back
to mother's house legless, armless, prone
only because fathers did before them,
all walls are wailing walls.

Walls raised to separate east
of sister from west of brother, beds
of dreamers, lovers, virgins, must
be toppled. Walls are the strongest things

we know, stout enough to bear the wind,
windows full of heaven, nights
of hunters, bear and swan, gourds
of moon, masterpieces of each dawn.

Refuge, siege, prison, sanctuary,
sight and blindness, law, law, law—
walls inscribe all human needs.
It only matters where we're made

to stand, how soon we need to leave.

Sister Mary Appassionata Addresses
the Psychic Research Guild
of Marion, Ohio

So much that could save us, solve us
the high muck-a-mucks won't let us near.
At Wright-Patterson A.F.B. in Dayton
in a maximum security hangar
guarded by vicious pinschers and pit bulls
and DNA-seeking death rays,
the air force has suspended
in liquid nitrogen three Venusians
whose saucer, disabled by acid rain
and fluctuations in the ozone levels,
came down hard on Route 71
midway between Akron and Cleveland.
The governor of the State of Ohio
and the adjutant general
of the Ohio National Guard know this
yet consistently ignore my letters
and fail to return my calls.
What are they afraid of?

Two out of every one hundred babies
born in the U.S. come into the world
wearing a tail; one in every ten thousand
arrives gilled, finned and scaled,
trailing oozy weeds from the primal sea
like clouds of glory; recently,
near Toledo a child was born
with wings, a white robe and halo.
All this is irrefutable evidence
for and against evolution.

Only art won't lie. We can read
even after desert aeons in statues and paintings
what ailed Amenhotep IV:

hyperpituitarism and T.B.,
hypergonadism, acromegaly (or perhaps
chromophobe adenoma), and,
it should be pointed out,
many many centuries of utter peace.

Women give off numerous
spiritual secretions which regulate
life and love, Eastern texts
assure us. In all, fifteen
have been named, but there's a sixteenth
which has been kept secret.
Why this conspiracy of silence?
What are men afraid of?

Let them fluoridate our water,
jam our brain waves
with their state-of-the art transmissions,
abuse our weather with flybys
of Io and Uranus.
We're saved, each night journeying
out of the body to go where we will,
each dawn born again into flesh
by the most human instinct,
this frantic lust just to believe.

Sister Mary Appassionata Lectures
the Urban Studies Class:
Gunfire, Bedroom, Passion's Trash

Can gunfire rattle like bone dice
in carryouts, motel rooms and bars;
sirens rise like startled city pigeons,
fumes from tired foundries over shattered faces
of the poor reflected on midnight rivers,
churn of burning urban currents, when we love?

Why, we ask, so much piggishness and rage
in bedrooms and kitchens, blood on the hands
of businessman, bureaucrat, citizen and priest?
Hate still hides itself in long white sheets,
earth ripped open to hide our every sin,
corpse after corpse borne to dust,

passion's trash.

Sister Mary Appassionata Lectures
the Journalism and Metaphysics Classes:
Who What Where When Why?

Moving down the crowded aisle, rush hour,
the No. 22 bus careening along Lorain Avenue,
potholed and congested, toward Cleveland's
downtown and an honest day's work, you think
you move due east, but everything you pass

hastens west, while the ancient planet
you inch across spins like a carny wheel
at the Cuyahoga County Fair, shifts like
the Tilt-a-Whirl with well-greased weight
of each and every season, running circles

around Old Sol, who too must spin, spin,
hustling through creation's eerie ether
while its Milky Way through other galaxies
pours like dregs of the pail's soapy water
emptied down the steepest gravel drive,

and for all you know this universe dances
like an Italian father drunk at his daughter's
wedding through a trillion others. In
the midst of such ceaseless velocities,
where's balance? Who can navigate for long

this labyrinth of parallax? When you've
used up all your day's light, soul and body
hurtling into night like a commuter train
twenty minutes late through a sudden tunnel
or a corpse swan-diving into earth's sea:

Just *who* do you think you are?
What will you come home to after all?

Where will you find yourself by dawn?
When did it hit you you were lost?
Now tell me *why*.

*Sister Mary Appassionata Lectures
the Biology Class: Natural Selection
and the Evolution of Fear*

After each day's light lumbers off
to wallow into extinction and we climb
into the foliage of our mammal sleep,
the winds of three dreams rise to chill us,
scents of the only three fears:
Darkness, Falling and Snake.
We recall the hankering for blood,
hearts howling at the fat moon,
stars beyond our limbs clustering
into myth. Fresh flesh quickens
the pulse, loosens tongue,
but words still choked back
to grunts, drowning in bitter froth.
One by one we reach in dream an inch
too far, night winds whistling a lullaby
in our ears, last song caught
in the throat. One terrible reptile
waits at the foot of each tree,
jaws opening on a greater dark.
Here's the enemy, since that dawn
we crawled ashore. Yet our fathers
offer a light bright enough
to burn such phantoms
from the most restless sleep.
They teach us to believe
living means never letting go
no matter how sweet the wood and fruit
of home, how great the urge to fly,
and falling, they say, must last forever.

Sister Mary Appassionata Lectures
the Quantitative Analysis Class:
Proof of the Existence of the Soul

For nine months weigh
everything you take in:
knowledge and refreshment,
medicine, love and wind.

Over the same period weigh
everything you lose: savor
of every word, signature
of each breath, mists of life.
The difference means your very soul.

Sister Mary Appassionata Quizzes
the Physics Class

What warns the circle
to stay away from corners?
Draws dusk from each dawn?

Reminds every hawk
the end of falling must
ever be to rise?

Tells scent and spore
love insists they give
themselves to every wind?

Warns each shadow
never to move between
a something and its light?

Sister Mary Appassionata
to the Home Ec Class

There is a popular conception that most nations have the cuisine they deserve.
  —Food in History

I.
Horace swore that a fat hen
drowned in finest wine tasted

something like love. Death's
the spice. Eating merely to live

renders us nothing but old bones,
blood pudding, meat tough

as year-old jerky. We must
rattle those pots and pans

to make a joyful thunder, frighten
off demons of deadly habitude.

Cooking's our art most spiritual
and earthy, unvarying good taste

made of fire and time. Hunger
means some dying, each bite and swallow

like each breath, a reprieve.
Along the ninth-century Rhine

ergotism taught the ravenous folk
how bitter could be their portions,

deadliness of this our daily bread,
in each crust twenty poisons, even LSD,

their bodies hot as ovens, a rash
of mad visions of the eternal place

we're remanded to, without hunger,
by the sentence most mortal:

For this is my body.

2.
Plant herbs and fruit trees
in the churchyard, one trunk
and patch of leafy fragrance

between each pair of graves
so the dead will serve to satisfy
your every hunger and the end

of rooting into clay and mire
of Mother Earth will be to rise,
root, bole, leaf to sweetest fruit,

one certain cure for each disease.

3.
Like a night of love
each meal must put to the test
all five senses. Life's
savor, what we thrust or suck
between the lips, touch to tongue
must be the kind of passion
worth dying for.
The Roman gourmand,
porcine Apicius—
when he realized he'd only
10 million sesterces left,
little less than one ton
of gold bullion, not near enough
to maintain his daily ache
for wild sow, belly bulging
with live thrushes,
and brain of peacock,
flamingo tongue, roe
of lamprey, livers of pike

caught precisely midway
between the Tiber Island
and the cloaca maxima—
reclined before a vial
of poison. It was,
he swore, just before
frothing, writhing
he lay down to sleep off
this Last Supper,
the most satisfying feast
he'd ever partaken of,
bitter and sweet as life itself.

Sister Mary Appassionata
to the Continuing Education Class:
The Singles Messiah Appears
in Columbus, Ohio

There's a fever on the wind,
in the blood. Don jumpsuits,
women, open to the navel
over clinging tube tops.
Let there be a riot of designer labels,
blush-on, bags and heels
too chic for words,
tan lines, coke lines,
Charlie and Tabu. Style
your hair, men, semi-Afro
or New Wave chop. Let chest hair
flourish, art rescuing nature
where necessary, balled-up sock
in Jockey briefs even,
shark's tooth necklace,
chains, chains, chains.
Know that nothing matters
but the music, Marvin Gaye to BeeGees.
You were made to do this dance,
strut your stuff
around life's teeming bar,
its intimate booths.
Mimic all things young and real.
Make eye contact. Hit
all the right lines. Small talk
only, please. Chablis. Perrier. Coors.
Whoever your partner, make sure
you get off first.
Don't even stay for breakfast.
The light of day's but the time
you're given to make ready
for an endless night.
When Judgment comes,

and it's coming soon, heaven
will be open all night long
only for the lost and lonely.

Sister Mary Appassionata Addresses
the Eighth-Grade Boys and Girls
during a Field Trip to the Museum
of Natural History and Art

The brittleness of what the world calls art!
Only bones, ochre and gold moans, frazzled weavings

dry as corn rows rustling in flaw-blown snow.
Rooms, rooms, rooms of stone. Nothing present

outlives its seer. All things fill and bleed,
rise to stumble, ignite to give their heat away.

What are we looking for we couldn't find studying
the backs of our hands as we write, labor or pray,

lines of care engraved around mother's eyes, portraits
hung in morning mirrors, plainsong of every last breath?

Sister Mary Appassionata Lectures
the Eighth-Grade Boys and Girls:
Flesh Willing, Spirit Weak

In some ways yes we're nothing but
our acts and deeds. Yet even more
we're all we haven't, what we've
done unwell, consequence of inaction:

the times we couldn't keep tongue
from singing another soul hurt,
gardens running to seed behind
too many ramshackle houses,

entire Library of Congress classifications
unborrowed or unreturned. Elections
where we abstained, resolutions
unadopted, suffering we backed

away from, grindstones it hurt
too much to keep the nose to,
days unseized, lovers spurned, times
flesh was willing but the spirit weak.

Sister Mary Appassionata
on the History of Heat

And at once a gentle fire has caught throughout my flesh.
  —Sappho

The old ones felt it as part
of every matter, *caloric,* to be
freed by alchemy or other fire,

but we've grown cold enough to see
the dance of meson on vector boson,
gaseous fire riling metal of the pot

to madden water just enough
to draw from reticent leaves tea's
utter wisdom, so real it hurts

lips and tongue to love, to speak,
so full of light our words are made
steam. Metal's the best conductor,

with electrons enough to spare.
The worst friend of heat? Nothing.
Ask any martyr, hater, lover, corpse:

flesh and bone conduct all too well.

Sister Mary Appassionata Lectures
the Photography Club:
Nothing We Can't See

In the beginning, sure as
too much light, darkness blinds,
but wait just long enough and night
brightens to a world we can see
well enough to dream ourselves
unold again, lovely as our parents
in their feverish wedding reel,
everyone we're kin to, their faces
looking down loving from the wall
whole again and incorrupt, ticks
of light and color whirling
into angels who orbit the bed,
everyone who loved us loving still,
elders, ash and pine whispering
secrets to stars just beyond
bedroom walls. When we're patient
with the dark it all takes shape
and we become a part of heaven,
our heavy selves an unjust law
no longer. We learn to fly.
In time there's nothing we can't see.

Sister Mary Appassionata
to the Human Awareness Class:
One Fate Worse

Loutish soldiers joke in line
outside the bamboo hut, khaki pants
draped over their arms, scream
after scream bursting from inside.
A mother; her two daughters,
twelve and nine. Knees
wrenched apart, clothing shredded
like newsprint. Or in the cities,
Saturday-night specials and shivs,
blasted glass glistening in arc-light,
lust blunt and beastly, big
as a fist. An old one
limp as Raggedy Ann lying
beside her bed on Social Security day,
seventy-five or eighty,
dollar bills and change, a few rings
worn smooth as baby skin strewn
over the floor, the invader's
footsteps clattering down stairs.
One fate's worse than death, in truth,
children, one red stain
on this scarlet earth
no god in his right mind could forgive.

Sister Mary Appassionata Lectures
the Ethics Class

Swear no oath to mean forever.
No one's made to stay so long,
and promise unfulfilled can leave
your children full of scorn
or bloated and pale in dust,
wounds blooming red as poppies.
Don't whisper to the deaf,
race any lame. Put no obstacles
in the way of the blind.
Leave gleanings in corners
of your fields to ensure
the poor be always with you.
The want of one widow or orphan
becomes your family hunger.
It's confusion to lie
with any beast or neighbor's mate
or with yourself while others
writhe in sleep alone.
What are hands for but to worship
or work, erect the house of love?
Care too much for nothing that can be
melted down. Take care
those appointed to feast on the goat
your sins have fattened are hungry
as the tribe was wrong.
In a world of strident wanting
leftovers can kill.
Know that all things count.
What you do, each gesture
of the hand, step, melody or word
can be only right or wrong.

Sister Mary Appassionata Lectures
the History Class: Doctrines of Memory

Not one of us recollects
the first nine months, two years,
when we were lamprey, toad,

lemur, ape. Ontogeny recapitulates
phylogeny—or is it the other way
around? Twenty-five million years ago

we all wore tails, and still today
we're born wagging the coccyx.
The blood never forgets. The bone.

Memory depends. It flavors
the being. Greatest wait. Just born,
what in the world can we recall

but sudden ache about the heart,
clasp, thrash of passion, dark sea
breathing all around, time's

tight squeeze, its gush, abrupt fall
to a netherworld, earth too bloody,
bright for words? It's then

we mark the gathering hurt, life-
long crescendo, fugue of age.
It never fails, sure as we're born,

life adds up until we're put
in a hole the sum of life's parts.
Count with me now: every moment

you were human, every one divine.

Sister Mary Appassionata
on the Nature of Sound

Sound is the least controllable of all sense modalities.
—Julian Jaynes

It's the sense that counts us human
more than any other. Though not
to touch can be our choosing,
veiling eyes, holding nose,
stiffened lips together tight
as the clam's in matters of taste,
try as we might ears can't be closed.

Who speaks our way, whether
to declaim *I hate you, love*
or merely *Good day to you,*
we've no choice but to let
into the mind, cede an instant
of our lives to seek to understand,
become a part of all we'll know.

Even could we declare ourselves gods
as did those crewcut Mach 1 boys
who first outflew all sound, most fear,
body's rumbling percussion even,
still there are voices heard within
that rasp and coo out terror, love,
fathers, mothers speaking their minds.

Sister Mary Appassionata Lectures
the Biology Class: Historia naturalis

The Master Designer's got a sense of justice; also
humor. Blue jays, raucous bullies of the treetops
mean and brutal enough to peck to death fallen nestlings
of weaker kin to gorge themselves on the innocence
of tiny eyes, over and over again are drawn to visions,
brilliant, gaudy monarch, yet can't stomach beauty

so pure, burning, retching pain forgotten the moment
such fluttering allure comes near again. There's
a lesson here, my children, to be read in the ranks
of leafy worlds above our own, whichever way the wind
blows. Starlings going north or south fashion
in their formations every letter of scripture,

chronicle of life's wish and striving, lust for light
that's purer still beyond the next horizon balanced
by the ache for home, the known. If you're too much
bothered by the persistence of flies, it's a sign
they're helping you bear in mind each instant
of their fragile lives what you're trying to forget:

sweet and meaty sense of the beast in you. Kill
one fly and two more arrive to sing its funeral.
Your own. God placed all wisdom and faith outdoors.
Walk into dawn's fields and woods with eyes and ears
open and there's nothing you won't know, nothing
you can't bring yourself to ache for and believe.

Sister Mary Appassionata Lectures
the Mortuary Science Class:
Feeding the Dead

Northern scapegoats hurled
into murky eternities of the bog
never were sent away hungry.
Mayan mortals were interred
with mouths stuffed with maize.

In graves of antique Greeks,
feeding tubes whereby survivors
once poured steaming broth
down between lips, over tongues
of their decomposing loves and dreads.

In Lagash a dead man entombed
with seven jars of beer, forty-seven loaves.
The dead wax bigger than life
to walk beside us, take hands
of our children through night mists.

No matter the season. They lie
with us time and again, each dream,
battening, thriving on the feasts
we living offer, the bitter and sweet,
all our art, this damned remembering.

Index of Poems